KEEPING SCORE

THE FIRST FIFTY YEARS OF THE CENTRAL STATISTICAL OFFICE

by

Reg Ward and Ted Doggett

Keeping Score
The First Fifty Years of the Central Statistical Office

Prepared by the Central Office of Information and the
Central Statistical Office,
January 1991. Printed in the UK for HMSO.
Dd 8240258, STATJ0014NJ.
© Crown Copyright 1991

ISBN 0 903308 02 9

KEEPING SCORE

THE FIRST FIFTY YEARS OF THE CENTRAL STATISTICAL OFFICE

by

Reg Ward and Ted Doggett

CONTENTS

ACKNOWLEDGEMENTS

In producing this historical account we have received an immense amount of co-operation. Firstly we thank the four directors for providing us or leaving us with a wealth of detail about developments under their tenure of office. We have received much help from colleagues in the CSO and ex-members of the office. Staff at the Department of Trade and Industry, Treasury, Cabinet Office and Department of Employment provided us with valuable assistance. Staff at the Public Record Office and the Royal Statistical Society also contributed to the research into this history. The book incorporates information from well over 100 sources. No attempt has been made to refer to sources in this book but the authors are willing to make available sources of information on request.

The aim of the book is to provide an illustrated history. For this a collection of photographs was required. We thank the Treasury for giving us access to the Lister Collection and DTI for making their photographs available. We are grateful to the *Sevenoaks Chronicle* for permission to reproduce material. We are also grateful to past and present members of the CSO and of Eurostat who provided photographs.

We also thank the Central Office of Information for providing editorial assistance and arranging for publication.

Finally our thanks go to Mrs Christine White who spent considerable effort putting this book in a form ready for publication. Her encouragement and organisation made the production task that much easier.

FOREWORD

BY THE
RT HON JOHN MAJOR

Rt Hon John Major.

T he importance of statistics is paramount to understanding the economy and society. They form the basis on which economic and social policy can be made. It is essential therefore that we get our statistics right. Throughout the short history of the Central Statistical Office there have been vast improvements. The state of CSO statistics has grown from its sparse beginnings in the dark days of 1941 to its fully comprehensive approach of today. This owes much to the four directors who have steered progress over the last 50 years. It is right to reflect where we have reached but we must note that there are still many imperfections in our statistics. We can look back on the 50-year history with pride but at the same time note the challenge that still exists for the CSO to improve its product further. I congratulate the CSO on reaching its 50th anniversary and I look to continued improvements in the future.

The Rt Hon John Major

CHAPTER I

INTRODUCTION

During the Second World War the Prime Minister, Winston Churchill, wrote to Sir Edward Bridges on 8 November 1940:

'Many of the executive Departments naturally have set up and developed their own statistical branches ...

It is essential to consolidate and make sure that agreed figures only are used. The utmost confusion is caused when people argue on different statistical data. I wish all statistics to be concentrated in my own branch as Prime Minister and Minister of Defence, from which alone the final authoritative working statistics will issue. The various Departmental statistical branches will, of course, continue as at present, but agreement must be reached between them and the Central Statistical Office.

Pray look into this, and advise me how my wish can be most speedily and effectively achieved.'

From this request consideration was given to the establishment of a Central Statistical Office. In a Cabinet minute dated 27 January 1941 a formal announcement was made to set up the CSO and shortly afterwards, Harry Campion was made director.

Initially the announcement made very little difference in practice. Harry Campion was a member of the Central Economic Information Service in the Cabinet Office under Josiah Stamp. He had been providing advice on statistical matters in 1940. When the CSO was established, Harry Campion's role continued as before. The requirements for the war effort took precedence over considerations about the newly created office. One of his early tasks was to get a team of statisticians together. There was a demand for statisticians capable of handling the descriptive data required for the war effort and for developing elaborate national income accounts. The latter reflected the economic work of assessing along Keynesian lines the use of resources in the war effort. Campion recruited some distinguished economic statisticians – Ely Devons, Ron Fowler, Richard Stone and Jack Stafford – who were brought into wartime government service. Two years later R H Coase, M R Fisher and many others had been added to their ranks.

The CSO was initially set up to service the war effort but it quickly established itself as a permanent feature of government. After 1945 there was an expansion in the work of official statisticians. This resulted mainly from the aim to manage the economy through controlling government income and expenditure with the use of an integrated system of national accounts. The passing of the Statistics of Trade Act in 1947 made it possible to collect more information from industry. Around this time statisticians were first recognised as a separate career category in the Civil Service. It was not long before demands to improve the timeliness of results were made. Harold Macmillan, then Chancellor of the Exchequer, said in his 1956 Budget speech that the figures were generally so far behind, that managing the economy was like trying to catch a train using last year's Bradshaw (which in the 1950s was the railway timetable). Improvements resulted with a system of quarterly national accounts introduced in 1958.

Comprehensive financial statistics were published first in 1962, following criticism by the Radcliffe Committee. More fundamental proposals were made in 1966 in the report of the House of Commons Estimates Committee.

In 1967 Sir Harry Campion retired. The second director of the CSO was Claus Moser, professor of statistics at the London School of Economics. It was his task to introduce the improvements recommended by the Estimates Committee. One recommendation was to introduce a more centralised system of collecting information from industry. For this the Business Statistics Office was set up in Newport and an integrated system of short period inquiries introduced.

There was progress not only on economic statistics but also on social statistics. The setting up of the Office of Population Censuses and Surveys enabled greater centralisation of social statistics. The annual publication *Social Trends* was introduced which brought together a wide range of social information in a co-ordinated framework.

In the 1970s there was a rapid growth in the number of statisticians working for government. For the whole of the Civil Service the number of professionally trained statisticians rose from 150 in 1966 to 550 in 1978. Within the CSO the increase was from 26 in 1966 to 60 in 1978. The Moser tenure of office was thus marked by a rapid expansion in the quality and coverage of statistics and matched by an increase in the complement of statisticians.

CSO's Directors, Sir Harry Campion, Sir John Boreham, Sir Claus Moser and Sir Jack Hibbert.

Sir Claus Moser retired as head of the CSO in 1978. His deputy at the CSO, John Boreham, took over the running of the office. A review of statistics, conducted in 1980, proposed greater emphasis on statistics required by government and less focus on statistics required by other bodies. Also with its deregulation policy the government wanted to ensure that the burdens imposed on industry by statistical forms were no more than was essential. As a result, the Government Statistical Service was cut by around 25 per cent. The CSO also took a proportional reduction, but continued to produce the same range of economic statistics and to carry out its central GSS functions.

In 1985 Sir John Boreham retired and Jack Hibbert became the fourth director of the CSO. During 1986 and 1987 it became increasingly apparent that the quality of the economic statistics produced by the CSO was inadequate. Among the reasons for this were the effects of deregulation and the rapid change in the structure of the UK economy. Statistics were slow to respond and quality problems became evident. In 1988 a review, conducted by Stephen Pickford, was undertaken. This led to over 30 recommendations for further research. More significantly, the review called for greater centralisation of work on economic statistics to ensure that priorities could be decided within an enlarged CSO.

As a result, in the middle of 1989 the Business Statistics Office at Newport, most of the two statistics divisions at the headquarters of the Department of Trade and Industry, and the statistics division working on retail prices and the family expenditure survey in the Department of Employment were merged with the CSO. The size of the CSO thus rose from under 200 to over 1,000.

This signalled the start of a new phase for the CSO. With the reorganisation in place an improvement programme was developed. In evidence to the Treasury and Civil Service Committee at the House of Commons, the then Chancellor of the Exchequer, John Major, indicated the need for improved statistics. He told the Committee that he had asked Sir Jack Hibbert for a programme of improvements focusing on the national accounts and the balance of payments. This programme of improvements was announced in May 1990 and was accompanied by an increase of around 100 staff.

This book expands the above history concentrating on the changes, the people involved and the outcomes. But our history starts prior to the establishment of the CSO in 1941. Why was a CSO not set up 50 or 100 years earlier? Some would argue that the only way of achieving an efficient, well planned and integrated statistical service is through complete centralisation. Such a system operated in Canada, Australia, Sweden, Germany, the Netherlands, Norway and many other countries. Few industrialised countries had a decentralised system as operated in the UK prior to the Second World War and indeed since then. The UK system, in which individual ministries have their own statistics departments, developed in the nineteenth and the early part of the twentieth century alongside the formation of departmental policy and decisions. Decentralisation has many advantages, especially to meet departmental requirements.

In Chapter II we take a look at the evolution of economic statistics since the early 1800s. In looking at this history we are conscious that there were several calls for the establishment of a CSO. The action taken in 1941 could have been achieved on a number of occasions in the preceding 100 years. The opportunity was there. Indeed, a decision to create a CSO was agreed in 1880 but was never implemented. The call for a CSO on these earlier occasions stemmed from concern about both quality and coverage of economic statistics.

The establishment of the present CSO in January 1941 is described in Chapter III. The events which led to its creation are given in detail and are based on the available public records of the event. The work of the CSO in the war years is described in Chapter IV. As the CSO was originally established to service the war effort, we explain some of the pressures in the 1940s to retain the CSO after the war.

With a new department, some expansion is to be expected as the Department finds its feet and as demands for its service increase. Chapter V discusses these pressures and introduces some of the personalities involved during the years to 1967 when Sir Harry Campion was director.

The expansion of the Moser years is described in Chapter VI. The reaction to the Estimates Committee is given in more detail while the establishment of the Business Statistics Office and the developments of the 1970s are considered. This is followed in Chapter VII by an account of the changes which occurred during the tenure of Sir John Boreham, the third director. The decisions which led to cut backs in

CSO Directors' meeting in 1990.

the CSO are explained. Sir Jack Hibbert's tenure as fourth director is described in Chapter VIII. It gives a fuller account of the developments which led to the reorganisation of the CSO in 1989 and its subsequent expansion.

The reorganisation of 1989 led to a merging with the CSO of the Business Statistics Office, most parts of the two statistics divisions of the Department of Trade and Industry located in London and part of the statistics division of the Department of Employment. In putting together the history of the CSO it is relevant to trace its family tree. In Chapters IX and X we look at developments in those areas which now are consolidated in the CSO. The history of the developments in statistics at the Department of Trade and Industry, in Chapter IX, is a continuation of the developments in economic statistics indicated in Chapter II – responsibility for the early development of economic statistics was largely the concern of the Board of Trade.

Finally we conclude by looking at some trends and developments that might affect the next 50 years of the CSO's history. Chapter XI assesses the current state of the CSO and considers the impact of emerging pressures and the influence which the development of statistics over the last 50 years might have on the future.

The statements made about statistics since 1960 are based on published material or contained in lectures given about the CSO by the four directors. These are necessarily selective but the authors consider all the statements made in the later chapters to be a true reflection of events during those years. They alone accept full responsibility for any errors or omissions.

Authors with Christine White. Ted Doggett on the right.

CHAPTER II

EARLY
DEVELOPMENT
IN ECONOMIC
STATISTICS

Official statistics in the UK before 1941 have a long and chequered history. Records relating to imports and exports go back to the seventeenth century. Other developments in official statistics since the beginning of the nineteenth century include: the first population census in 1801; the start of the collection of statistics of births and deaths in England and Wales in 1837; the first census of earnings in 1886; the first census of production in 1907; the first cost of living index in 1914; the first index of production in 1928; and the first official estimate of national income in 1941.

It was in March 1753 that a bill was presented to Parliament on the Annual Count of the People. The bill met with considerable opposition and the proposal was viewed with such alarm that it was rejected by the House of Lords. In the ensuing years there was much debate about the size of the population in England. It was the underlying supposition in Thomas Malthus's 'Essay on the Principle of Population as it Affects the Future Improvement of Society, 1798', that there was an increase. Other researchers maintained the opposite. Around this time another bill for a census of population of Great Britain was under consideration by Parliament and in 1801 the first decennial population census took place. The population of Great Britain was nine million. There was no central authority for the control of census operations. The census was carried out in England by overseers, acting under Justices of the Peace, and High Constables. In Scotland it was undertaken by village schoolmasters, while Ireland was excluded from the bill.

Conditions for the evolution of statistics were in many respects favourable in the early nineteenth century. The modernisation of government made it easier to compile statistical information and the prejudice against publication of statistical documents began to disappear. Statistics were also influenced by the advances made in methodology.

The beginning of the 1830s saw a growth in official economic statistics. Statistical institutes were founded, numerous statistical societies sprang up and statistical journals were started. From very early times, the collection of trade statistics had been a function of the Board of Trade, but until 1832 the Board was not equipped with the means to analyse and present the trade figures obtained from Customs. The trade figures did not reach a wide public.

Before 1832 the Board collected *ad hoc* statistics to help in investigations referred to it, for example the treatment of American shipping under the navigation laws. Following the enactment of the Corn Return Acts of 1789, the Board of Trade was involved in the collection of information relating to corn prices and stocks. Their collection was continued long after the Corn Laws were repealed.

The development of statistics at the Board of Trade in the early 1830s owed much to a paper by William Jacob in 1830. He was the Comptroller of Corn Returns at the Board. Jacob indicated:

'Little statistical information has been collected, and that chiefly by the industry of the two Houses of Parliament, but that little has been so mingled with a vast mass of irrelevant, or unimportant, or tiresome details, and is scattered through such a

The Rt Honble
T S Rice —

Board of Trade
31st March 1832.

Sir

I am directed by the Lords &c to request that you will submit to the consideration of the Lords Commrs of His Majesty's Treasury the following proposal for establishing in this Department, a Branch, the Duties of which shall be, to obtain and systematically arrange Returns upon the Wealth, Commerce & Industry of the United Kingdom for the purpose of preserving Information, and, from time to time, of publishing such Reports as have generally been required by Parliament, or by His Majesty's Govt —

No System for carefully abstracting in clear and accurate Form, the Information which passes through the Board of Trade on these subjects has yet been established, & it appears to the Lords of this Committee that a distinct Branch for this Purpose, obtaining Returns from other Departments, and concentrating the Information already in their Possession, might be of great public Utility, & although attended with some Expense, yet, that indirectly the saving to the Public upon the costly & desultory Returns which are occasionally called for, by the Houses of Parliament would be considerable.

Their Lordships would propose that the vast mass of Statistic Information which is contained in the Returns to Parliament for the last Ten years should be digested & concentrated under separate Heads so as to be of easy reference, & to establish a Form under which a complete and extended System may be periodically carried on — Happily a portion of the Labour necessary to this object has been anticipated by private Industry; and the difficulty will not be great — Beyond this, it can be only necessary, on the present occasion, very shortly to recapitulate the further means of Information which might be placed at their disposal.

The Excise would give a measure of that consumption which marks the general distribution of Wealth & Comfort in the Country with some View by means of the *number of ponderous folio volumes, that it has presented an appalling labour to all but the most indefatigable inquirer.'*

Jacob's paper led to demands for a statistical department at the Board of Trade. A case was presented to the Treasury who agreed with the need for good information and also the value of savings made by rationalisation.

In 1832 the statistical department was set up. The president of the Board, Lord Auckland, first gave an invitation to Charles Knight to 'digest the information contained in Parliamentary Reports and Papers'. Charles Knight was editor of the

George Richardson Porter.

Companion to the Almanac. He declined Lord Auckland's offer but recommended George Richardson Porter for the post. In 1831 Porter had contributed an essay on life assurance in the *Companion.* Porter was born in 1792 and was married to the sister of the famous economist Ricardo. He had failed earlier in business as a sugar broker.

George Porter's appointment in April 1832 was on a temporary basis. His objective was to arrange and make abstracts from Parliamentary Returns. Soon after taking up his appointment the proposal that a Central Statistical Office be set up was made. The Parliamentary Select Committee on Public Documents considered the best means of providing information 'with a view to Economy, facility of Access and clearness of Arrangements'. Its major recommendation was the extension of the Board of Trade statistical department in order to create a Central Statistical Office. The recommendation was not carried out because of conflict over who should head the office.

On 31 January 1834, Porter was given an established position as superintendent of the statistical department with a salary of £525 rising by annual increments of £25 to £600. His salary was raised to £800 in 1838.

Porter instituted a type of statistical year book under the title of *Tables of the Revenue, Population, Commerce, etc of the United Kingdom and its Dependencies.* He took over the running of the Railway Department in 1844 as well as continuing to run the statistical department.

The *Account of Trade and Navigation*, often popularly described as the 'Board of Trade returns', originated slightly earlier, having been first presented to Parliament in 1830 under the name of Mr Courtenay, the vice-president of the Board of Trade. They were hence known as the Courtenay Tables. Porter incorporated these tables into his statistical year book.

Around the time Porter was setting up his department, statistical societies were being formed in Great Britain and Ireland. Most prominent of these was the Statistical Society of London, founded in 1834. The preceding year a Statistical Society of Manchester was formed. Several others appeared in the 1830s, in Ulster, Liverpool, Glasgow, Leeds and Bristol. There was a tendency to create statistical sections in scientific societies. At a meeting of the British Association for the Advancement of Science in Cambridge in 1833, a statistical section was formed. Its meeting in 1836 in Bristol gave rise to the Statistical Society there.

Many motives may have led to the foundation of these societies but a major factor was an acute interest in social problems. The volumes of the journals of the statistical societies amply testify to an interest in the education of the poor. Other topics were also of interest. For example, the London Society tried to collect material relating to strikes. It also formed a committee for vital statistics and another for criminal statistics.

In his statistical work at the Board of Trade Porter was helped by Rawson Rawson and Richard Valpy, who were appointed assistants in 1842. In the 1840s there was much criticism of the annual tables. Their main fault was their apparent aimlessness in that everything was printed that came to hand. In 1845 there appeared a particular set of annual tables on crime in Manchester, down to the amount of

Rawson Rawson.

money taken from drunks by police and returned to them when sober, the number of public houses with musical entertainment and the number of public houses licensed to keep billiard and bagatelle tables.

In 1847, Porter was promoted to joint permanent secretary in the Board of Trade. The importance of statistical work in the government's mind may be gauged from the fact that when a replacement was needed for the promoted Porter in 1847, the man chosen was Albany Fonblanque, a man who had no statistical experience.

Albany Fonblanque was born in London in 1793. He was educated at Woolwich. His parents had intended that he joined the Royal Engineers

First Annual Abstract of Statistics.

FOR THE

UNITED KINGDOM

In each Year from 1840 to 1853.

(TO BE CONTINUED ANNUALLY.)

Presented to both Houses of Parliament by Command of Her Majesty.

LONDON:
PRINTED BY GEORGE EDWARD EYRE AND WILLIAM SPOTTISWOODE,
PRINTERS TO THE QUEEN'S MOST EXCELLENT MAJESTY.
FOR HER MAJESTY'S STATIONERY OFFICE.

1854

CONTENTS.

Note.—The figures for the year 1853 may be subject to future revision, owing to final corrections in the Public Accounts.

STATISTICAL DEPARTMENT, BOARD OF TRADE,
Whitehall, March 1854.

A. W. FONBLANQUE.

but this was not followed, on account of a long illness. In 1830, Fonblanque ran a paper called *The Examiner*. His writings in *The Examiner* brought a following from John Stuart Mill, Disraeli and Carlyle. In 1847, when the Liberals were returned to office, Fonblanque consented to relinquish the editorship of *The Examiner* and accepted the appointment, apparently most uncongenial to a wit and satirist, as head of statistics at the Board of Trade at a salary of £800. Fonblanque had also been offered the governorship of Nova Scotia but he could not tear himself away from London. He felt entirely out of place as the Board of Trade's statistician. There were many reports of his late arrivals, his early departures, his panics when called upon for official information and his general inaccessibility. Undoubtedly it was his assistant, Richard Valpy, who took the major role in securing the output of the office.

It is evident that Fonblanque had upset Disraeli in some of his articles in *The Examiner*. Disraeli, soon after Fonblanque had taken up his post at the Board of Trade wrote:

'... *the Office of the Chief of the Statistical Department held by Fonblanque, an imbecile as a man of business and who passes his official hours in writing libels against us, should be suppressed and its supervision transferred to its proper superintendent, the Commercial Secretary of the Board of Trade. It would be a delightful arrangement turning him out. We should save £800 per annum and when we read his abuse of us in* The Examiner *we would have the satisfaction of knowing that we had done something for the distinction.*'

Porter died in 1852 at Tunbridge Wells. The cause of his death was 'a gnat's sting on the knee'. His views on free trade in the Board of Trade had become so notorious that Disraeli remarked that his death 'was occasioned, I suppose, by the accession of a Protectionist Ministry'.

In 1854 under the direction of the Board of Trade's reforming president, Edward Cardwell, the whole set of statistical publications was recast. From that year dates the first publication of the *Statistical Abstract of the United Kingdom*. This is still published today under the title *Annual Abstract*. In 1855, the Board of Trade published the *Annual Statistics of Trade* and in 1856 the first of the triennial *Volume of Colonial Statistics* appeared. Also in 1856 *Miscellaneous Statistics of the UK* appeared for the first time and remained in circulation until 1879.

Most of these volumes were compiled by the statistical department using information from other Departments. It appeared that the Board of Trade was acting as a central statistical department at that time. The coverage of information extended to the whole field of economic statistics and was by no means limited to the subject matter dealt with by the Board of Trade.

In 1854, the relative responsibilities of the Board of Trade and Customs and Excise for statistics on trade and navigation gave rise to a difference of opinion. Originally both trade statistics and navigation statistics were compiled by Customs, while the Board of Trade exercised supervision over the statistical forms and presented the results to Parliament. With the overhaul of statistical work in the Board of Trade in 1854 the task of compiling the navigation

Lavers Coffee House, 1850. This site is now occupied by the CSO in Great George Street.

returns was transferred, after a Treasury inquiry, to the statistical department at the Board of Trade. Customs continued to compile the returns of foreign trade.

External trade statistics were much criticised in the 1860s. At the request of the Board of Trade, the Statistical Society of London set up a committee on the subject in 1869 and organised a conference with city merchants. The committee reported in 1870. This led to establishment of the Statistical Office of Customs and Excise in 1871. The arrangements were still not completely satisfactory and in 1876 a proposal was discussed, though not adopted, for transferring the whole responsibility for supervision from the Board of Trade to the Treasury. The difficulty was resolved by the creation of a joint committee consisting of the chief statistical officers of the Board of Trade and Customs to deal with questions of principle affecting trade statistics and to revise annually their form and content in accordance with the changing requirements of trade. The joint committee was advisory only.

In 1871 Frederick Purdy, the head of statistics at the Poor Law Board, commented on the fragmented and unco-ordinated nature of official statistics. He called for the setting up of a Central Statistical Office. His concern arose from:

> '... the absence of authority of seeing on behalf of Parliament that its orders for statistical returns are properly fulfilled.'

He argued for forming a department which would be an intermediary between Parliament and the various government Departments which collected statistics.

Fonblanque died in office in 1872. He was replaced for one year by Lack and then in 1874 by his assistant, Valpy. The early 1870s was a troubled time for economic statistics with great concern about their quality. Against this background came the appointment of Robert Giffen as head of the statistical department at the Board of Trade in 1876. Robert Giffen was born in Strathaven, Lanarkshire in 1837 and like Fonblanque he was a journalist. He started his career as an apprentice to a lawyer in Strathaven. In 1860 he became a reporter and sub-editor on

the *Stirling Journal*. Two years later he moved to London as sub-editor on the *Globe*. He then joined the staff of *The Economist*. He was assistant editor from 1870 to 1876. He was also city editor of the *Daily News* from 1873.

A question that had already given rise to a difference of opinion was the extent to which statistics should be centralised in one department or dealt with in each administrative department in close connection with the subject matter. Giffen was a strong advocate for centralisation, not only within the Board of Trade, but also within the government service generally. He sympathised with the idea of constructing a central statistical department to service the requirements of all Departments of State.

Giffen's views were soon to be tested. Friction continued between the Board of Trade and Customs and the quality of economic statistics did not improve. These considerations were examined by an 'official statistical committee'. A Treasury minute signed by Mr W H Smith in 1877 appointed a committee to look at the open dispute on the trade statistics and the organisation of statistics more generally. Mr Childers (who later became Chancellor of the Exchequer) chaired the committee. Other members were Colonel Romilly, Commissioner of Customs; Mr Farrer, Secretary of the Board of Trade; Mr Welby of the Treasury; Mr Shaw Lefevre MP, Mr A J Balfour MP and Sir M W Ridley MP. The Treasury minute appointing the committee stated:

> '*My Lords have before them a correspondence with the Boards of Trade and of Customs upon the subject of the control to be exercised by those*

Departments respectively over the returns of trade and navigation of the United Kingdom which are annually presented to Parliament. The immediate question raised in this correspondence is one only of Departmental interest, and might no doubt be easily settled by a reference to the report upon the statistical branches of the Customs which was made to the Treasury in the year 1870 by Mr Shaw Lefevre and Mr Foster; but on considering this question my Lords have been led to observe that it forms only a part, and a very small part, of a much larger subject, which seems to call for serious attention: This is the compilation and publication by government Departments of statistics generally. My Lords have before them a memorandum upon this subject drawn up by Mr Lack, late assistant in the statistical branch of the Board of Trade and another, prepared by Mr Giffen, now head of that Department, both of which show that there is great room for improvement in the system on which official statistics are prepared.

Indeed, it can scarcely be said that at present there is any system at all. Each Department compiles and publishes from time to time information more or less detailed with regard to the business with which it is concerned, but there appears to be no fixed principles laid down for the guidance of the several offices, and the consequence is that with little harmony or coherence existing between the various classes of statistics thus published, comparison between them is often impossible, and their practical utility is thereby most seriously impaired. Perhaps no better proof of this is required than the fact that in connection with bills or motions in the House of Commons

returns are constantly being moved to supply information which is already before Parliament in official blue books, but which is there so embedded in masses of detail that it is no wonder members shrink from the labour of extracting it for themselves.'

The committee reported, in 1878, on the Departmental quarrel between the Board of Trade and Customs. Later in the same year the committee reported on the vast number of financial years used for annual returns of taxation. It was at the end of 1879 that the report on the main subject of their reference was made. In this last report, which was published in 1881, the committee stated that the unsatisfactory condition of official statistics was due:

(i) to the attempt to make information presented to Parliament serve the double purpose of continuous public record and of temporary instruction to administrators and departmental officers;

(ii) to the absence of any central or general supervision of national statistics regarded as a whole.

While the records show that the proposals of the committee were carefully examined by the government and to some extent adopted, it is significant that the two main recommendations made by the committee were never put into force. In the first of these it was proposed that:

'while each of the "statistically important" Departments should continue to be responsible for its own statistics, a small central statistical department, subordinate to the Treasury, should be set up with functions such as the preparation of annual abstracts, the compilation of an annual index of returns presented to Parliament, and the editing of a miscellaneous volume containing statistical returns from the smaller Departments'.

The second of the principal recommendations was:

'that after a preliminary survey of the statistics of all Departments, with a view to securing uniformity of system, a small permanent board or commission should be appointed to carry on the supervision of statistics and to secure continuance

of order and harmony in the general body of returns presented to Parliament'.

The recommendation to establish a small central statistical department, had it been adopted, would have amounted to little more than the transfer of certain activities of the Board of Trade to the new department. A member of the committee, Mr T H Farrer, then permanent secretary of the Board of Trade, dissented from the two main recommendations. In discussing the defects in official statistics, Farrer pointed out that it was important to recognise the causes, among which he included 'difficulties in the laws, customs and circumstances under which the different statistics are collected by different Departments and in different parts of the Kingdom'. He went on to say that:

'these differences and many others lie deep in the laws and customs of the three Kingdoms, and it would be sanguine to hope that they could be removed in order to render statistical records uniform. Human life and habits can seldom be altered in order to make records perfect.'

In addition to the objections made by the Board of Trade, Mr Gladstone, then the first Lord and Chancellor of the Exchequer, feared that such a central Department might extend its functions beyond the limits required at once by economy and expediency. So the recommendation to form a Central Statistical Office was rejected.

In the last 20 years of the nineteenth century, there was a marked growth of interest in social questions and on the state of the labour market.

This led to an important addition to the scope

of statistics at the Board of Trade. On 2 March 1886 on the motion of Charles Bradlaugh, the House of Commons adopted a resolution to the effect that full and accurate labour statistics should forthwith be collected and published. As a result Mr John Burnett, formerly general secretary of the Amalgamated Society of Engineers was appointed 'labour correspondent' at the Board of Trade. Under his auspices the collection of statistics on strikes, lock-outs, trade unions and the state of the labour market was started. At the same time the statistics department at the Board of Trade carried out a first attempt at a census of wages.

By the beginning of 1893 the work of collecting statistics and other information with regard to labour conditions was further developed and extended. A separate branch, known as the Labour Department, was created for this purpose within the Commercial and Statistical

Department under Giffen. More labour correspondents were appointed and a monthly *Labour Gazette* was started to give up-to-date information on issues such as employment, disputes and wages.

Further developments in economic statistics occurred after the turn of the century. In 1903 the Labour Department published a report on Wholesale and Retail Prices. The series for wholesale prices was taken back to 1871. In 1906 the statistical duties of the Board of Trade were greatly increased by the passage of the Census of Production Act which imposed on the Board the duty of taking at suitable intervals a census of industrial production in the United Kingdom. All officers taking part in the census and having individual returns were required by the Act to take an oath of secrecy. The first census was taken in 1908 with respect to production in 1907.

At the time the first census of production was

being considered there was another call for setting up a Central Statistical Office. This time the case was made by Sir Charles Dilke. Dilke pointed out in his presidential address to the Royal Statistical Society in 1907 that there had been little improvement in economic statistics since the Treasury Committee on Economic Statistics reported in 1880. New statistical departments had been created, such as those at the Board of Agriculture and the Board of Education, which made available 'more or less independently a considerable mass of Parliamentary statistics'. Also, statistics in other Departments were 'totally independent of each other and possessing but imperfect knowledge of the work upon which other offices have been and are engaged'.

Dilke gave a vivid account of the defects of UK economic statistics. These were similar to those considered by the Treasury Committee a quarter of a century earlier. He laid the blame partly on Parliament for asking for returns without considering what was the extent of the information they required and whether it was already accessible to them. He partly blamed Departments for not impressing on Ministers the need for uniformity and the necessity of amending legislation to secure uniformity. The state of confusion was such as to lead to distrust of most public statistics. Sir Charles Dilke stated:

'It may be as confidently asserted now, as it was by William Newmarch in 1869, that any Chancellor of the Exchequer desiring to reform our whole system of taxation would find himself without the necessary statistical equipment for the task.'

The remedy for the failings of statistics was considered by Dilke to be an institution of a general direction by a central Department. The issue was taken up before the House of Commons Select Committee on Publications and Debates in 1909 in evidence given by Sir Henry Rew. The Select Committee, after hearing the evidence, came to the conclusion that the subject was not within their terms of reference.

It was not long before another call was made for a Central Statistical Office. In 1915, Geoffrey Drage presented a paper to the Royal Statistical Society on 'The Reorganisation of Official Statistics and a Central Statistical Office'. Drage summarised the chief causes of the unsatisfactory condition of official statistics as:

(i) Lack of co-operation between different Departments.

(ii) The absence of any central or general supervision of national statistics as a whole.

(iii) The attempts to make the Blue Books, annually presented to Parliament, serve the double purpose of continuous public record and of temporary instruction to administrative and Departmental officers.

(iv) The inclusion in Departmental reports of quantities of matter for the purpose of showing how much work has been done in the year.

(v) The fact that compulsory powers are too few and too seldom applied.

(vi) Defective supervision in the collection of statistics and the employment, especially for census work, of ill-paid, uneducated and therefore uninterested persons in the collection.

Drage saw the remedy as a new central authority above that of Departments under the Prime Minister. He obtained substantial support for his views at the meeting of the Royal Statistical Society from two eminent economic statisticians, Arthur Bowley and Josiah Stamp, who would continue to press for a Central Statistical Office for many years.

Geoffrey Drage did not let his concern for the quality of economic statistics wane. He led a campaign for improvement which resulted in a petition signed by a number of statisticians, businessmen and others being presented to the government in November 1919. The main signatories to the petition were Geoffrey Drage, the Rt Hon Herbert Samuel, Professor Arthur Bowley, Mr A Waterlow King, and Dr Josiah Stamp. The petition was signed by some 20 members of the House of Lords and over 30 members of the House of Commons.

The petition listed the defects in statistics as those which Drage had mentioned in his address in 1915 to which was added that there was 'inadequate financial provision for the collection of essential statistics'. The petition went on to list the types of statistics that were inadequate. These included statistics on wages, incomes, production, railway traffic, trade between England and Ireland, number of trained seamen, number of houses and the consumption of food, clothing and other necessities.

The petition ended:

'Your petitioners submit that the questions raised

in this memorial are of sufficient importance to justify an immediate inquiry by a Royal Commission or Parliamentary Committee, and they suggest that such a commission or committee should forthwith be appointed to inquire into the existing methods of the collection and presentation of public statistics and to report on the means of improvement.'

The petition, sent to the Prime Minister, David Lloyd-George, was considered by the Cabinet in 1920. A committee was set up to inquire into the defects alleged in the petition. The committee was chaired by the government actuary, Sir Alfred Watson. Its members consisted of Sir George Beharrell, Ministry of Transport; Mr W Coates, Board of Inland Revenue; Mr Flux, Board of Trade; Mr M Heseltine, Ministry of Health; Mr Hilton, Ministry of Labour; Mr Rae, Treasury; Mr Reade, Customs; Mr Rose, Scottish Office; and Mr Vivian, Registrar General.

The committee reported in 1921 that:

'we have found that the underlying object of the petitioners, namely, that a central statistical department should be created with over-riding authority over other Departments, charged with the duty of supplying the public with statistical information not only in relation to the Departmental activities of the government but on all questions of general interest, would both extend the functions of government and alter the constitutional balance of governmental machinery.

On the desirability of extending the functions of government, we have not felt called upon to

REPORT

ON THE

COLLECTION AND PRESENTATION

OF

OFFICIAL STATISTICS.

PREPARED BY A COMMITTEE APPOINTED BY
THE CABINET.

LONDON:
PUBLISHED BY HIS MAJESTY'S STATIONERY OFFICE.
To be purchased through any Bookseller or directly from
H.M. STATIONERY OFFICE at the following addresses:
IMPERIAL HOUSE, KINGSWAY, LONDON, W.C. 2, and 28, ABINGDON STREET, LONDON, S.W. 1;
37, PETER STREET, MANCHESTER; 1, ST. ANDREW'S CRESCENT, CARDIFF;
23, FORTH STREET, EDINBURGH;
or from E. PONSONBY, LTD., 116, GRAFTON STREET, DUBLIN.
1921.
Price 1s. Net.

express an opinion, but we have pointed out that the provision of official statistics other than those essential for administrative purposes has been in the past subjected to well-defined limitations, determined by the national value of the statistics required, the cost of the collection and compilation, the nature of the inquiries necessary, and the views of the public as expressed in Parliament. Within these limitations a large and valuable body of official statistics has grown up, and we are confident that, when the dislocation caused by the war has been overcome, official statistics will be raised by existing or projected arrangements to a materially higher standard than was attained before the war. Moreover, an examination of the specific defects mentioned by the Petitioners has convinced us that the allegations put forward against the system of national statistics as it stands today are, broadly speaking, not established.'

The committee concluded:

'We are satisfied that while the existence of a Central Statistical Office would give rise to constitutional and other difficulties it would do little if anything to remove the conditions which at present limit the production of national statistics. These conditions would apply to a central office no less strictly than they do to existing Departments.'

The committee also recommended that for the purpose of ensuring more effective co-operation and co-ordination between the different Departments in their statistical work, a permanent consultative committee of statistical officers should be established. The consultative committee was given no powers to make recommendations to a central authority (Cabinet Office or Treasury) nor to receive direct representations from non-official statisticians or organisations. The consultative committee met occasionally in the 1920s under the chairmanship of the government actuary. There were a number of reports which criticised the consultative committee, and it was generally regarded as an ineffective body.

Calls for improvements in statistics came throughout the 1920s and 1930s. First the Balfour Committee, 1924–27, and then the Macmillan Committee in 1931 urged for better coverage. In April 1935 Roy Glenday read a paper to the Royal Statistical Society on 'The Use and Misuse of Economic Statistics'. He gave a severe criticism of the quality of official statistics. He complained that the public had to rely on casual collections of information. Official statistics, he claimed, could be subdivided into:

(i) Information collected for internal administrative purposes.

(ii) Information collected by government Departments for the service of their clients, for example local government.

(iii) General information demanded by Parliament and the general public.

Glenday indicated that these all had one common feature – that statistics were required for specialised and limited purposes; they were not intended to be contributions to a general national statistical service. Indeed in the mid-1930s there were no official national accounts. The only comprehensive national accounts were being compiled by Professor Bowley at the London School of Economics. Glenday proposed the setting up of a national statistical organisation.

About the same time the Manchester Statistical Society had set up a committee to consider the sufficiency of official statistics. The committee comprised Bernard Ellinger, Harry Campion (who later became the first director of the Central Statistical Office) and H G Hughes. Their memorandum indicated severe defects in the coverage of official statistics. The committee pointed out that:

(i) No official information was available regarding wholesale and retail distribution in the United Kingdom.

(ii) Nothing was known of the trade between Great Britain and Northern Ireland.

(iii) The amount and kind of goods carried by road could only be roughly estimated.

(iv) Figures of the changes in profits of different industries could be published without risk of disclosing the accounts of individual companies as many of the essential figures were already collected by the Board of Inland Revenue.

(v) A great deal more statistical knowledge was needed on banking and finance (as given in the report of the Macmillan Committee).

Ellinger, Campion and Hughes tried to get support from the Royal Statistical Society and other national organisations likely to be concerned and to organise a joint approach to the government.

The call in the 1920s and 1930s for improvements in economic statistics and the setting up of a Central Statistical Office was met with only a token response mainly concentrated on expanding the scope of industrial statistics. The outbreak of the Second World War saw proponents for change like Josiah Stamp and Harry Campion brought together in the team supporting the War Cabinet. It is of interest to speculate on their role in the decision to set up a Central Statistical Office in 1941 to meet the need of Sir Winston Churchill and the War Cabinet for undisputed figures relating to the war effort.

CHAPTER III

ESTABLISHMENT
OF CSO

By any judgement, the year 1940 must be regarded as one of the most perilous in British history. In the early part of the year Hitler's Germany had successfully invaded the countries of Europe. By July Britain stood alone in Europe, and a series of mass daylight air raids began, aimed at her sea ports. Following the success of the RAF in the Battle of Britain in August, the enemy turned to mass night-time raids – the blitz – on London and other industrial areas. It may seem strange that in a period of such pressure the Cabinet would give time and effort to the creation of a statistical office, with no responsibility for giving policy advice and no responsibility even for the direct collection of statistics. Its role was to be in essence co-ordination. To understand the pressures which led to this Department being set up we need to go back to the period just before the outbreak of the war.

The government had been preparing for a war for some time. In June 1939 the Chancellor of the Exchequer, Sir John Smith, presented a paper to the Cabinet entitled 'Survey of War Plans in the Economic and Financial Sphere'. Following Cabinet discussion a continuous Survey of Financial and Economic Plans was set up under the chairmanship of the noted economist and economic historian, Lord Stamp.

Josiah Stamp was the archetypal self-made man. He was born in 1880, the third son of a Kilburn shopkeeper, and the eldest to survive infancy. When Josiah was sixteen his father became ill and he left school to join the Civil Service as a clerk in the Inland Revenue. While working his way up through the ranks of the Civil Service by day, he was preparing himself for an external BSc (Economics) degree at London University in the evening. At the age of 38 he moved into the private sector. By 1939 he was president of the London Midland and Scottish Railway, a director of the Bank of England, chairman of the London School of Economics and a member of the government's Economic Advisory Council. The previous year he had been created Baron Stamp of Shortlands in Kent, in recognition of his many public services.

The other members of the Stamp Survey, as it became known, were 56-year-old Henry Clay and 49-year-old Hubert Henderson, both distinguished economists, and a senior civil servant, Francis Hemming, the secretary and chief administrator of the Survey. Hemming had served with distinction in the Army during the First World War, until he was severely wounded. He was invalided out in December 1918 and joined the Civil Service, where he enjoyed an equally distinguished career. In 1939 he was a principal assistant secretary in the War Cabinet offices, and secretary to the Economic Advisory Committee. In private life he was an expert on butterflies, and had written several papers for the Royal Entomological Society.

POLITICAL FLOODLIGHT.

In 1931 Josiah Stamp was seen as a man of some influence in the financial world. In this Low cartoon he is pictured bottom right, next to Montague Norman, Governor of the Bank of England.

Cartoon in the *Evening Standard*, 5 September 1931

Lord Stamp.

Service (CEIS), whose purpose was to provide the Stamp Survey with the economic and statistical material on which to base its work. In December 1939 the CEIS was set up as part of the War Cabinet Office staffed by a small group of economists and statisticians recruited from the universities.

Among the first to be conscripted to the new service was 34-year-old Harry Campion from Manchester University, who was to help to organise the statistics needed for the Stamp Survey. Some time later he recalled:

'I soon found I had a job to do. On my first day in the Cabinet Office I was asked about figures of employment in the engineering industry. Should they ask the Board of Trade or the Ministry of Labour for them? When I told them the figures they wanted were already there in the Ministry of Labour Gazette, I was told that there was no copy of the Gazette available in the Cabinet Office but it would be ordered. So I went out myself at lunchtime and bought a copy at the Stationery Office in Kingsway. The copy the office ordered arrived a week later!'

Campion was well suited by experience to set up a new statistical organisation. After leaving university he was in at the beginning of the Cotton Trade Statistical Bureau, an organisation which served the whole cotton industry by collecting figures on output and sales, and also assembling data on the cotton industries of other countries and principal export markets of particular relevance. The Bureau published a regular digest of statistics for the industry, and in doing so was able to make use of the expertise of

The function of the Survey was to examine from an economic viewpoint the plans made by Departments in anticipation of war, check for inconsistencies or deficiencies, and report to the Chancellor. This involved such diverse subjects as the mechanisms for price control, rationing, the utility clothing scheme and many others.

On 3 September 1939 the United Kingdom declared war on Germany. The Prime Minister, Neville Chamberlain, appointed a small War Cabinet containing nine members. A month later, following criticism in the House of Commons and in the press, two committees on economic policy were created - a ministerial committee chaired by the Chancellor of the Exchequer, and an official committee chaired by Lord Stamp.

By November, Stamp had prepared a paper on priority policy for his committee. On the basis of this the committee approved proposals for the establishment of a Central Economic Intelligence leading professionals in typography and layout in Manchester firms.

After a few years, Campion returned to Manchester University to set up an Economic Research Section. Much relevant applied research was done in the Section. An early example was a joint project with Professor Bowley of the London School of Economics under the auspices of the National Institute for Economic and Social Research (NIESR) to compile estimates of the national income of the United Kingdom for the years 1924 to 1938. Later, in 1940, these were to be updated by the CEIS and formed the starting point for development by Meade and Stone (see below) of what are now called the national accounts.

A priority for the statistical section of the CEIS was to arrange for copies of the main statistical series produced by Departments to be sent to the CEIS so that monthly summaries could be prepared to give a comprehensive and up-to-date picture of the developing economic situation. Before these summaries could be produced, however, there was a change of government. Winston Churchill became Prime Minister, at the head of a coalition government.

One of the first decisions made by Neville Chamberlain after the declaration of war was to reappoint Winston Churchill as First Lord of the Admiralty. One of Churchill's first decisions was to appoint Professor F A Lindemann as his personal adviser. The 53-year-old Lindemann had an extremely distinguished record at Oxford, both in physics research and as head of the Clarendon Laboratory.

At Oxford he was known as an abrasive, sarcastic individual, a reputation which was to be increased by his activities in government. Yet those close to him spoke warmly of his loyalty, his affection and his sense of humour. He was a man of frugal tastes. A lifelong vegetarian who neither smoked nor drank, he did not impose his views on others. Indeed, in minutes to Churchill during the war he argued against proposed restrictions on the production of beer on the grounds of its effect on the morale of the people. Winston Churchill met him for the first time in 1921 and, despite the difference in their tastes, there developed between them a warm mutual friendship and respect. One quality Lindemann had which served Churchill well during the war years was his ability to simplify quite complicated topics into a note which was short, yet complete in its essentials.

Although at first his function was to provide advice on scientific matters, he was soon asked by Churchill to form a statistical branch – 'S' branch

Professor F A Lindemann, later Lord Cherwell.

– to collect and collate statistics and to brief Churchill not only on naval affairs, but also on wider matters of which as a member of the War Cabinet he needed to be aware.

In May 1940 the coalition government took office. Convinced of the importance of reliable statistics, and of the value of professional interpretation of the figures, Churchill brought his statistical section with him to the Prime Minister's Office, where it became known as the 'Prime Minister's statistical section'. A prominent part of the work of the section was to chart for the Prime Minister the main statistics relating to the war effort. Nevertheless, the scope of the section's work was very wide, ranging from assessment of the scientific details of weapons development to statistical and economic matters. Sir Donald McDougall was Lindemann's right hand man in the section, and subsequently chief economic adviser to the Treasury. He later analysed the minutes submitted by Lindemann to the Prime Minister during the war and estimated that something approaching one third of the minutes related to non-scientific topics. Of these non-scientific minutes:

'perhaps 30 per cent were mainly concerned with the armed forces, 20 per cent mainly with shipping, 15 per cent with goods, agriculture and raw materials, about 10 per with post-war problems and the remaining 25 per cent with miscellaneous topics ranging widely from the building programme to the shortage of matches, from economic warfare to the supply of doctors, from Russia and India to export policy, rationing, inflation and austerity.'

The critical scrutiny of Departmental statistics was not always readily accepted. In the summer of 1940 the Air Ministry and the Ministry of Economic Warfare had estimated from production figures that Germany had a vast superiority in bombers. Lindemann argued over several months that this could not be so. In the end he applied the Air Ministry's methods to our own aircraft production and showed that it grossly overestimated the current strength. The Departments were hard to convince and in the end Churchill called in a high court judge, Mr Justice Singleton, to examine the available figures. His verdict supported Lindemann's view. Lindemann also concluded that the accuracy of British night bombing was much less than the Air Ministry claimed. He persuaded the Prime Minister to arrange for one of his staff to examine all the photographs of night bombing taken in recent months. The analysis showed conclusively that only a third of bombs were landing within five miles of their target – a staggering report which led to immediate action by the Prime Minister.

Other Departments were also affected by the way their statistics were taken and interpreted without consultation. An annoyed official of the War Office wrote on 27 September 1940:

'The Prime Minister's idea seems to be that Professor Lindemann is to spy around and get information he wants without allowing Departments to know what the information is to be used for. In this way the Prime Minister imagines that he will be able to penetrate the facade erected by each Department to hide their

misdeeds. Everything the Professor puts to the Prime Minister is kept secret from everybody else and is used for confronting people at meetings.'

The secretary to the War Cabinet, Sir Edward Bridges, tried to ease the situation by inviting Departments to appoint liaison officers within the branch, who would be allowed to examine any statistics prepared from data supplied by their Department.

But problems continued to emerge with the statistics supplied to Cabinet, and on 8 November, Churchill sent the following minute to Bridges:

Many of the executive Departments naturally have set up and developed their own statistical branches, but there appears to be a separate statistical branch attached to the Ministerial Committee on Production, and naturally the Ministry of Supply's statistical branch covers a very wide field. I have my own statistical branch under Professor Lindemann.

It is essential to consolidate and made sure that agreed figures only are used. The utmost confusion is caused when people argue on different statistical data. I wish all statistics to be concentrated in my own branch as Prime Minister and Minister of Defence, from which

War cabinet, 1941. Standing on the left is Sir Edward Bridges, Secretary to the War Cabinet. Seated are members of the cabinet [from left to right]: Ernest Bevin (Minister of Labour), Lord Beaverbrook (Minister of Aircraft Production), Anthony Eden (Foreign Secretary), Clement Attlee (Lord Privy Seal and Deputy Prime Minister), Winston Churchill (Prime Minister), Sir John Anderson (Lord President of the Council), Arthur Greenwood (Minister without Portfolio), and Sir Kingsley Wood (Chancellor of the Exchequer).

alone the final authoritative working statistics will issue. The various Departmental statistical branches will, of course, continue as at present, but agreement must be reached between them and the Central Statistical Office.

Pray look into this, and advise me how my wish can be most speedily and effectively achieved.'

It would appear that the 'statistical branch attached to the Ministerial Committee on Production' referred to the CEIS. The War Cabinet had set up five ministerial committees of which only the chairmen were members of the Cabinet. They were the Production Committee (or Council) and the Economic Policy Committee, both chaired by the Minister without without Portfolio, Arthur Greenwood; the Food Policy Committee and the Home Policy Committee, both chaired by Clement Attlee, Lord Privy Seal; and the Lord President's Committee, chaired by the Lord President of the Council (from May to 3 October, Neville Chamberlain, and from then on, Sir John Anderson), whose objective was 'to ensure that the work of the five ministerial committees is properly co-ordinated, and that no part of the field is left uncovered'.

Bridges' reaction to Churchill's minute was that there was in practice little duplication between the two statistical sections, but that the underlying problem was that some Departments had not got a systematic statistical organisation generating regular returns. They relied on *ad hoc* returns usually hurriedly compiled and often inconsistent with data previously supplied. The Prime Minister agreed that Sir Edward Bridges

should form a committee to sort things out. As a consequence, on 27 January 1941 the Central Statistical Office was born. The official announcement, issued with the Prime Minister's authority, included the following:

'2. A Central Statistical Office is being established, whose duty will comprise the collection from government Departments of a regular series of figures on a coherent and well ordered basis which cover the development of our war effort. The Prime Minister has directed that the figures so collected should form an agreed corpus which will be accepted and used without question, not only in inter-Departmental discussion, but in the preparation of documents submitted to Ministers for circulation to the War Cabinet and to War Cabinet Committees. This section, which will take over the work of issuing

Front page of WP(G) (41)12, the secret notice which formally set up the CSO.

(THIS DOCUMENT IS THE PROPERTY OF HIS BRITANNIC MAJESTY'S GOVERNMENT.)

S E C R E T.
W.P.(G.)(41) 12.
27th January, 1941.   COPY NO. 68

WAR CABINET.

CENTRAL STATISTICAL OFFICE AND ECONOMIC STAFF.

        The Prime Minister has approved the following revised arrangements for the central collection and presentation of statistical material and economic reports.

        (Signed) E.E. BRIDGES.

        1.   Revised arrangements for the organisation of Civil Committees were set out in the Prime Minister's Minute of the 30th December, 1940, (W.P.(G.)(40) 338). The following changes are notified in the present arrangements for the central collection and presentation of statistical material and economic reports.

        2.   A Central Statistical Office is being established, whose duty will comprise the collection from Government Departments of a regular series of figures on a coherent and well ordered basis covering the development of our war effort. The Prime Minister has directed that the figures so collected should form an agreed corpus which will be accepted and used without question, not only in inter-Departmental discussion, but in the preparation of documents submitted to Ministers for circulation to the War Cabinet and to War Cabinet Committees. This Section, which will take over the work of issuing statistical digests hitherto performed by the Economic Section of the War Cabinet Secretariat, will form part of the staff of the War Cabinet Offices.

        3.   The Prime Minister's Statistical Branch under Professor Lindemann will, as heretofore, be responsible for analysing and presenting to the Prime Minister all statistical information which he requires and it will be the particular duty of Professor Lindemann and his Branch to warn the Prime Minister to the best of their ability, as Minister of Defence, and through him the War Cabinet, of any pending shortages or discordances in our war effort.

-1-

statistical digests hitherto performed by the Economic Section of the War Cabinet Secretariat, will form part of the staff of the War Cabinet Offices.

3. The Prime Minister's Statistical Branch under Professor Lindemann will, as heretofore, be responsible for analysing and presenting to the Prime Minister all statistical information which he requires and it will be the particular duty of Professor Lindemann and his Branch to warn the Prime Minister, to the best of their ability, as Minister of Defence, and through him the War Cabinet, of any pending shortages or discordances in our war effort.

4. Under the Prime Minister's minute of 30 December, the Lord President's Committee have taken over consideration of the larger issues of economic policy. A staff of economists, will in future be a separate body from the staff engaged on preparing statistical digests (see paragraph 2), will be put at the disposal of the Lord President's

Ely Devons, a founder member of the CSO.

Committee for the preparation of such special reports as may be required. Individual members of this Economic Staff (which will be attached to the War Cabinet Office) may also be detailed to provide studies of special subjects as may be required from time to time for other War Cabinet Committees; in particular, the Import and Production Executives, and the Committee on reconstruction problems under the chairmanship of the Minister without Portfolio.

5. The Economic Survey, under Lord Stamp, will be discontinued as such. At Sir John Anderson's request, Lord Stamp has agreed to

Ronald Fowler, a founder member of the CSO.

Professor A L Bowley, responsible for pre-war estimates of national income.

Richard Stone, who with James Meade produced the first official estimates of national income.

place his services at the disposal of the Lord President, as and when required, in connection with the economic side of the work of the Lord President's Committee.'

The announcement added that the CSO would 'have the assistance of' a small advisory committee comprising representatives of the Prime Minister's statistical branch and three or four of the chief statistical officers of the Departments mainly concerned with statistical matters. Thus the CSO was hived off from the Central Economic Intelligence Section, and in continuing the work of producing statistical digests for the Cabinet, started by Harry Campion in CEIS, it pursued questions of consistency, coherence, and accuracy. Not least among its functions, though not explicit, it formed a buffer between Lindemann and the Departmental collectors of statistics.

The original CSO, in early February 1941 comprised Hemming, the administrative head, and seven statisticians and a support staff of 16 clerks and typists, which they shared with the Economic Staff (later known as the Economic Section). The names of several of the statisticians will be familiar to those who work in economic statistics. They were: Campion, Meade, Devons, Fowler, Stone, Joan Marley and Sally Chilver. Within a month Hemming was transferred, and Harry Campion at the age of 35 became head of the CSO, a position he held until his retirement in 1967.

The creation of the CSO greatly widened the scope of its interests. No longer confined to statistical questions raised in the economic policy committees, its responsibility was to agree the

THE GAP

The 1941 Budget, seen through the eyes of Low. From the portrait, Montague Norman is watching the Chancellor, Kingsley Wood, trying to bridge the gap between the resources required to fight the war, and those available.
Cartoon in the *Evening Standard*, 7 April 1941

basis of all statistics brought before the War Cabinet, and to ensure that where the quality of the figures was inadequate the Department took steps to rectify the situation. The developments over the war years are described in Chapter IV. Initial work was, naturally enough, a continuation of that done in the CEIS.

Two series of statistical digests were produced. Series A was prepared at the request of the Lord President's Committee, and provided information on the output of munitions, industrial production, shipping, labour, food, raw materials and foreign trade in summary form for Ministers. It was first issued in June 1940. Series B was a more detailed document giving the chief figures used for inter-departmental discussions at both official and ministerial level. Topics included production, machine tools, consumption, stocks, labour, prices, finance, transport, shipping and foreign trade. Series B was the precursor of the *Monthly Digest of Statistics*.

Another development of continuing importance which began at that time was the production of official estimates of national income. In 1940 the CEIS had updated Bowley's pre-war estimates for 1938 and presented them to the Stamp Survey. The committee decided that a full survey was necessary. In the summer of 1940 James Meade and later Richard Stone began drawing up the plans. Richard Stone quoted two sources of inspiration for their work, Colin Clark's *National Income and Outlay* (1937) and Keynes' classic *How to Pay for the War* (1940).

The search for statistical building blocks to put together the first official estimates of national income and expenditure was difficult. Some of their suppliers were sceptical of the value of the exercise but most were sympathetic and helpful. Meanwhile the press debated whether drastic measures would be necessary in the coming Budget to finance the war. Since the general view seemed much more pessimistic than the picture emerging from the CSO work, the Treasury (in the form of Sir Richard Hopkins and Lord Keynes) decided that publication would be highly desirable. The Chancellor of the Exchequer agreed, and when he opened his Budget he presented to Parliament a new White Paper, Cmd 6261 *An Analysis of the Sources of War Finance and an Estimate of the National Income and Expenditure in 1938 and 1940*. It was to be the first of a long line of White Papers and Blue Books. The numbers had been assembled by James Meade and Richard Stone, and the text had originated with Lord Keynes.

CHAPTER IV

THE WAR
YEARS

The new Central Statistical Office was given a wide remit in that it was to be responsible not just for statistics relevant to the economic progress committees, but for all statistics (except those on operational matters) being prepared for Cabinet committees.

The first duty of the office was to ensure that the statistics needed for the monitoring of current developments were being provided regularly by the Departments concerned, and were being produced on a reliable and suitable basis. Figures put forward without the imprimatur of the CSO were unlikely to receive the unquestioning acceptance of other Departments that the Prime Minister wished. When Departments had agreed with the CSO about the kind of statistics that were needed it was incumbent on the CSO and the Departments to ensure that reports to Cabinet committees consistently and properly used these figures.

Of course, expansion of activity by the CSO was restricted by the resources available. By 1943 its size had increased to 44, of which 17 were graduate statisticians or economists, and 27 support staff. By that time, the output of the Department had increased phenomenally.

Instead of two series of monthly statistical digests they were producing six, with quarterly and annual supplements to series B. They were also producing 13 more detailed and specialised weekly, monthly and quarterly statements and the annual national income White Paper. This is all the more impressive when one realises that even if the basic data were supplied by another Department, each revised figure had to be transcribed by hand, checked, sent to the printer and the results proof-read. A list of the statistical statements being prepared regularly by the CSO is shown in the Annex.

The preparation of national accounts had become a regular institution. The governments of the Dominions and the United States had decided to produce similar estimates, with the help of our experts.

By 1943 the CSO was providing a statistical service to the Economic Section, to the North American Supplies Committee (a committee which was concerned with co-ordinating the production of munitions for the United States and the United Kingdom, and co-ordinating their allocation to the two countries' forces) and had taken responsibility for the highly sensitive business of obtaining statistics from Departments for the Prime Minister's statistical branch. It was also preparing special statistical reports either independently or in collaboration with Departments, for the War Cabinet and Cabinet committees. It was the focus of all liaison and collaboration between Departments on statistical matters.

The Central Statistical Office had a special role with regard to the United States. Just as it was important for the Cabinet not to have to argue about the statistics it received, it was important that our ally should receive statistical information that was clear and unambiguous. All statistics to be sent to the United States went via the CSO, where they were vetted to ensure that they had been compared on the agreed basis. All statistical information from the United States also came through the CSO, so that it could be disseminated efficiently to those who needed to have it. The CSO was also responsible for arranging with the United States Government

"That pepper castor is the Axis, see? And this mustard-pot is us. These nuts are enemy U-boats, and now, just here —— by the way, I s'pose you haven't got a spare nutcracker about you?"

EXPLAINING IT TO HARRY HOPKINS

Harry Hopkins was President Roosevelt's special envoy in the UK. Britain's needs were in reality expressed not by nutcrackers but by the CSO's statistical reports to the North American Supplies Committee.
Cartoon in the *Evening Standard*, 13 January 1941

Pedestrians in Whitehall running for shelter at the sound of the air raid siren, 1939.

Air raid damage to the Treasury, October 1940. An earlier picture of the building appears in Chapter II. The war damage revealed Tudor remains on the site.

Departments the production of joint statistical statements in a common form and on the basis of similar definitions to be used in the two countries. Examples of such statements related to munitions output, raw materials, shipping and munitions assignments, are listed in the Annex.

The CSO also acted as a central body for the collection of information from the Dominions, the Colonies and the British Empire on such questions as strengths of the Armed Forces, casualties and munitions production. Arrangements were made for estimates of the national income and expenditure of the British Dominions to be compiled in similar form to the United Kingdom estimates.

The latter, which were prepared by the CSO in collaboration with the Treasury, were considered by the Budget Committee. Summaries of the results were published at the time of the Budget in the White Papers on war finance and national income and expenditure.

The Central Statistical Office also:

(i) acted as a clearing house for information on changes in forward munition programmes on behalf of the Ministry of Production, the Supply and Service Departments and the Offices of the Minister of Defence.

(ii) acted, when requested, as a central organisation for the discussion of statistical questionnaires proposed to be issued to employers and other bodies by government Departments, for the collection of information for general inter-departmental use.

(iii) maintained relations with private and semi-public organisations outside the government which were engaged in statistical inquiries and prepared statistical information used by government Departments. In particular, it had relations with the National Institute of Economic and Social Research, the Bank of England and the universities. These external relations were to become important for post-war development.

To perform these duties, the Central Statistical Office had to build up an entirely new organisation. This task was made all the more difficult since, by the beginning of 1941, there was an acute shortage of trained statistical personnel available. The kind of organisation which was developed was one designed to make the best possible use of the expert knowledge of its specialist staff and to relieve them, so far as possible, of day-to-day administration.

The Cenotaph lit by incendiaries, 1941.

Almost all the senior staff of the Office possessed high university qualifications in statistics and economics, and before the war had been members of university staffs. Before joining the Central Statistical Office they had already established reputations in the conduct of statistical investigations. This staff of specialists were allocated work in particular fields, such as national income, food, raw materials, shipping and munitions. Their duties included:

(i) The maintenance of day-to-day liaison between the Offices of the War Cabinet and the statistical divisions of each Department. All figures for inclusion in statements prepared for Cabinet committees or issued by the Central Statistical Office itself were normally agreed between them and the statisticians of the Department concerned.

(ii) Keeping fully informed of all problems of policy within their field of study, as well as in the changing methods of compilation to ensure the statistics were relevant and the interpretation of them reliable and useful.

(iii) The development of new methods of statistical analysis for the problems encountered in their fields of work. The outstanding example in the period was the national income and expenditure work, where data from various sources on incomes, expenditure, savings and stocks were brought together in a social accounting framework and each adjusted on to a basis that was consistent as far as possible with each other, and with the macro-economic concepts on which they were focused.

In order to give the greatest possible flexibility in the organisation to meet special emergencies, members of the staff were transferred, as occasion arose, from one field of study to another with the aim that all the specialist staff would have practical experience in the handling of figures of at least two or three Departments.

The organisation of the Central Statistical Office in March 1943 was as follows:

Section A (General)

This section was responsible for:
(i) Production of all statistical statements issued from the Office
(ii) The supervision of:
(a) Pool of statistical assistants from which assistants were allocated to specialists for special work;
(b) Computing pool;
(c) Charting section.

Section B (Civil)

This was subdivided into:
(i)   Food and agriculture
(ii)   Industrial production and raw materials
(iii) Shipping
(iv)   Manpower (civil)
(v)   Manpower (Armed Forces)
(vi)   Coal, fuel and light
(vii) Supplies to Allies
(viii) Petroleum products
(ix)   Enemy resources
(x)   Post-war reconstruction

Section C (Military)

This section was concerned with British,

American and Empire production, and stocks of munitions and warlike stores, subdivided as follows:

(i) Naval construction
(ii) Ground equipment
(iii) Aircraft

Section D (National Income and Finance)

This section was responsible for the work done on national income and expenditure, home and overseas investment, balance of payments, public income and expenditure and savings.

The head of the Central Statistical Office was responsible to the secretary of the War Cabinet for the work of the Central Statistical Office, consulting him on all questions of policy. The

Advisory Committee met three times in 1941, but there is no record of any subsequent meetings.

Obviously, the Central Statistical Office could not have carried through its work unless it maintained the most friendly relations with the statistics divisions of all Departments. Shortly after the Office was formed, discussions took place with Departments for the purpose of establishing effective working relations. These arrangements, although they had of necessity to be slightly modified from time to time, were in general as follows:

(i) In order to ensure that statistics presented to Cabinet committees were agreed between Departments and the Central Statistical Office, each Department would send regularly to the

Barbed wire and sandbag barricades being built around the Great George Street building, facing Birdcage Walk. Note the iron gates, since removed.

Office copies of their main statistical reports. Thus, the CSO maintained a complete and up-to-date collection of all statistical returns collected by government Departments. If a Department used statistics relating to production, employment, shipping, or other subjects in a paper to a Cabinet committee, these statistics could be checked immediately and their meaning and coverage readily established from the returns already made available to the Central Statistical Office. Many of the reports prepared by the Departments were of a MOST SECRET nature, but there was an undertaking that the CSO should not pass to any other Department

Plaque outside Norfolk House.

Norfolk House was bombed in December 1940. The damage cannot have been as serious as it looks, for the CSO was in occupation 16 months later.

Norfolk House in 1990.

figures sent for record purposes without having the prior consent of the originating Department.

(ii) While the Central Statistical Office took the responsibility of ensuring the Departmental figures were used so far as possible by the War Cabinet and its committees in a manner satisfactory to the originating Department, the CSO encouraged the statistics divisions of Departments to assert their influence within their own Departments to maintain statistical standards. This was perhaps the first example of many through the years, of statisticians in Departments accepting on an informal basis the obligation to co-operate with the CSO. Without such co-operation, many of the advances made over the last 50 years would not have been possible.

The original office occupied by the early economists and statisticians seconded to assist with the war effort was in Richmond Terrace. By the middle of 1940 the War Cabinet Office expanded into part of the New Police (Curtis Green) Building. At this time the 'Central War Rooms' were being built on the lower ground floors in the Great George Street building. Shortage of accommodation was so acute that much of the CSO had to be housed in other buildings. The office was accommodated in parts of Church House (Dean's Yard), Gwydyr House, Audit House (Embankment) and Norfolk House (St James Square).

The CSO was not the only occupant of Richmond Terrace and Gwydyr House. The files held at the Public Record Office testify to serious matters relating to another occupant as the following correspondence describes.

16 June, 1939

Dear Mr Burden,

I have been asked to obtain authority for the issue of an allowance of 5/- per month for the upkeep of the office cat at Gwydyr House. The present holder of that position has been carrying out his mice-killing functions there since August last, when the building was re-occupied, and has hitherto been supported by the cleaners there.

The Cabinet Office cat, for which an allowance was authorised in Pyle's letter no. T.G.247/01 of 17th July, 1936, condescends to grace by his presence both of our buildings in Richmond Terrace. Being just a cat, and therefore without any sense of gratitude towards the hand that feeds him, I'm afraid he could not be induced to extend his sphere of action to cover Gwydyr House, and so save the state 5/- per month!

I should be glad if the new allowance could be agreed to.

Yours sincerely,

S F Rawlins

S.F. RAWLINS

R.H. Burden, Esq.,
TREASURY, S.W.1

OUR DUMB FRIENDS LEAGUE HOSPITAL

ECCLESTON STREET, S.W.

This is to certify that 'Jumbo'
(War Cabinet Mouse Exterminator) is
suffering from "Eatoomuchitis" and is
unable to follow his employment.

I.C. Blood

(Signed) I.C. BLOOD
Date: 3/6/42 Veterinary Surgeon

OUR DUMB FRIENDS LEAGUE HOSPITAL

ECCLESTON STREET, S.W.

This is to certify that 'Jumbo',
the War Cabinet Mouse Exterminator, passed
out of all his nine lives on 8th June, 1942.

Complaint: None at all! It leaves the
mice quite cold!

I.C. Blood

(Signed) I.C. BLOOD
Veterinary Surgeon

Mr Crudass

Mr Davey

Mr J. Umbo, a member of staff who has given
frequent service in this Office, has lost his lives.
A death certificate is attached. This casualty
should be recorded in our CAT-alogue of Events
during the War.

Please take up with the next-of-kin (the
Supt. of Cleaners) the disposition of the allowance
which has been paid from Public Funds towards the
upkeep of the deceased. It is understood that he
left some dependents (number unascertainable), and
that his widows are probably left unprovided for.

The question of a replacement for Mr Umbo is
being taken up with Feline Headquarters.

S F Rawlins

S.F. RAWLINS

10.6.42

MR CRUDASS

Major Rawlins has instructed that, owing to the shortage of males, in consequence of the War, the vacancy for the position of Mouse Exterminator in this Office, caused by the decease of Jumbo, should be filled by a female feline.

An applicant, name and pedigree unknown, at present unofficially employed in the Canteen, offers herself as a candidate. Her qualifications for the position are somewhat obscure, but it is known that her enthusiasm and ability for increasing the feline population in this locality is very great, and it is suggested that her services in this direction might be more appreciated by, and acceptable to, the Ministry of Production.

S L Heath.

S.L. HEATH
Office Keeper
10.6.42

MAJOR RAWLINS

May the appointment date from 19th June 1942, please.

AH Crudass

A.H. CRUDASS
12.6.42

An Analysis of the Sources of
War Finance and an Estimate of the
National Income and Expenditure
in 1938 and 1940

*Presented by the Financial Secretary to the Treasury to Parliament
by Command of His Majesty
April 1941*

LONDON
PRINTED AND PUBLISHED BY HIS MAJESTY'S STATIONERY OFFICE
To be purchased directly from H.M. STATIONERY OFFICE at the following addresses:
York House, Kingsway, London, W.C.2; 120 George Street, Edinburgh 2;
26 York Street, Manchester 1; 1 St. Andrew's Crescent, Cardiff;
80 Chichester Street, Belfast;
or through any bookseller

1941
Price 3d. net

Cmd. 6261

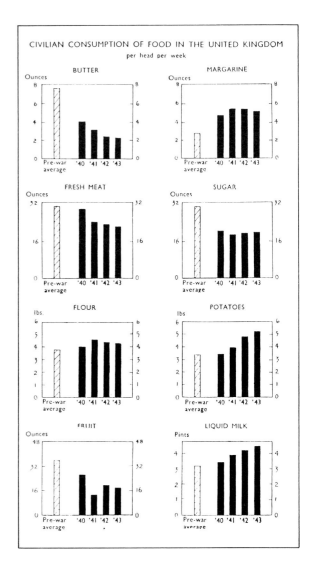

46

CHAPTER V

THE CAMPION
YEARS

Sir Harry Campion.

T he pre-war attitude towards the collection of statistics was extremely restrictive. In the words of a Royal Statistical Society memorandum published in 1943:

'... no Department possessed general powers to collect such statistics as it might require. The Registrar-General's Department had the duty of conducting the population census and of doing such current work as the recording of births and deaths. The Board of Trade conducted a census of production and the Ministry of Agriculture an annual agricultural census, both under statute. Of course, the Revenue Departments had certain powers to require certain information necessary for the performance of their functions. But in all of these cases the scope of the questions which might be asked was carefully limited and the legislation concerned seems to have been drafted with a view to protecting the individual against having a Department prying into his personal affairs.'

We have seen how the CSO was brought into being in the early days of the war to meet very specifically war-based objectives; to provide an unambiguous data base of statistics on which the crucial decisions of the war could be based. We have seen how it built up comprehensive statistics of the resources of the nation, in terms of munitions, production, manpower, at a time when all of those resources had to be directed towards the aim of winning the war.

Now we look at the pressures that led to a change in the pre-war attitude, and the birth (or rebirth) under Harry Campion of the major

economic statistics that today form most of the output of the enlarged Central Statistical Office.

By 1943 the tide of war had turned. The nation was confident that the Allies would eventually win, and many people turned their minds to the policies of the post-war world. The previous year, Beveridge had produced his report on social security. As far as statistics were concerned, the Royal Statistical Society was the first to go public. In October 1942 they had set up a committee under the chairmanship of Professor Major Greenwood, including Hector Leak of the Board of Trade, and such eminent statisticians as R F George, M G Kendall, E S Pearson and E C Snow. Sir George Epps, the government actuary, also attended. Their brief was to 'consider and report upon the organisation of statistics in government Departments before, during and after the war, with special reference to:

(i) the staffing of Departments
(ii) the relationships between Departments
(iii) the advantages and disadvantages of alternative schemes of post-war organisation.'

Their report was the *Memorandum of Official Statistics*, published in 1943. They observed that much beneficial co-ordination had been done during the war, and would need to be continued in peacetime. They identified three new areas of co-ordination. First, in the status and influence of statisticians, who they believed should be treated on a par with the graduate entry administrative class. Second, there was a role for the CSO in the development of statistical methods within government. Finally the CSO should be an influence for the introduction of up-to-date mechanical methods of data handling within the Civil Service.

The memorandum recommended that the co-ordination of statistical work should be effected by the Central Statistical Office operating through a small committee selected from the heads of Departmental statistical branches.

Statisticians, even the Royal Statistical Society, could have been thought of as interested parties when the future of statistics was being discussed. However, the government was also alert to the potential of economic statistics as a tool of economic planning. There was a widespread conviction that the swings in unemployment that had occurred in the inter-war years were, with the right policies, avoidable, and should not be allowed to happen again. By the end of the war, the White Papers on National Income and Expenditure had established their place in the annual Budget preparations. The Budget was no longer merely a government housekeeping exercise; it was an attempt at macro-economic management. Lord Woolton, occupier of many ministerial posts during the war, and Minister of Reconstruction in 1944, was to write:

Sir Edward (later Lord) Bridges.

'The proved competence of the statistician, both in the field of financial forecasts and in the operations of government in wartime, has given much stimulus to those who believe in what, in broad terms, is called National Planning, and in particular to its use in preventing some of the economic waste and personal tragedy that has been an accepted part of our social life in the past.'

Business also favoured the provision of more statistics. In April 1945 a group of prominent firms in manufacturing and distribution wrote to the Chancellor pressing him to resume publication of statistics of overseas trade and production, and to publish more of the detail underlying the national income and expenditure figures. The group included such household names as Cadburys, Courtaulds, Dunlop, Lever Brothers, Lyons and Imperial Tobacco. The Chancellor wrote a sympathetic reply, stating that the whole question of government statistics was under review; that every effort would be made to resume publication by Departments of their statistics after the war was over; but pleaded a shortage of manpower which might make it impossible to resume publication immediately.

In July 1945 *The Economist* published its prescription for the CSO:

'If it is to perform efficiently its task of illuminating economic policy, the Central Statistical Office will require much fuller statistical information than was available before the war; in other words, it will feel most keenly the deficiencies of existing statistical services ... By reason of its task, it will have to press for more statistics, for greater frequency in collection and speed in assembly, and for uniformity of classification.'

The Economist concluded that:

'Good statistics are far more important to a country whose economic policy proceeds by guiding and assisting industries and firms whose decisions are free, than to one that operates through an imposed plan, just as an accurate chart is more necessary for a ship sailing the free seas than to a car driving down a concrete highway. The businessman, who will have to provide the facts asked for, can rightly insist that he should not be troubled unnecessarily or by too many overlapping Departments. But if he is wise, he will regard the efficient collection of statistical information as one of the chief safeguards against the totalitarian state.'

The question of the future of the Central Statistical Office was settled officially on 7 March 1944 when, in an arranged Parliamentary

EMPLOYMENT POLICY

Presented by the Minister of Reconstruction to Parliament
by Command of His Majesty
May 1944

LONDON
HIS MAJESTY'S STATIONERY OFFICE
ONE SHILLING NET

Cmd. 6527

The White Paper on Employment Policy (Command 6527).

Question, Mr Molson asked the Chancellor of the Exchequer 'whether he will give an assurance that the Central Statistical Office, which is now collecting a very wide range of statistics relating to financial activities of the country will be retained as a permanent institution after the War?' Sir John Anderson's reply was 'Yes sir. It is intended that a Central Statistical Office in some form shall be part of the permanent machinery of Government after the war.'

But who was to head the CSO after the war? Most of the academics who had been conscripted in for the war were to return to their universities. It had been agreed, at the request of the first Secretary General of the United Nations, Mr Trygve Lie, that Harry Campion should be seconded to the United Nations for a year to organise the birth of the statistical office of the newly formed United Nations Organisation. Manchester University were impatient for him to return to fill a professorial chair. But in the mind of the Cabinet Secretary, Sir Edward Bridges, there was only one candidate. 'Go back to Manchester, if you must,' he told Campion. 'But don't write in complaining about the quality of official statistics. You are the man we need.'

So Harry Campion stayed on. Jack Stafford deputised for him the year he was at the United Nations, while Hector Leak was prevailed upon to delay his retirement from the Board of Trade until Stafford was able to take over. Campion's stint at the United Nations was by no means an unprofitable one for the CSO. It established the CSO at the forefront of the development of official statistics internationally as well as at home. The cross-fertilisation with the ideas of statisticians from other governments was to prove fruitful in our domestic developments.

The widespread conviction that the national economy could and should be managed much better after the war led the coalition government to issue in May 1944 a *White Paper on Employment Policy* (Command 6527). This influential document stated that 'the government accepts as one of their primary aims and responsibilities the maintenance of a high and stable level of employment after the war', and detailed the methods by which this could be attained.

From the viewpoint of the development of government statistics this White Paper was important in that it spelt out in detail the statistics considered necessary to conduct the policy of full employment. It said:

'The following are the principal classes of statistics (in addition to those available before the war) which must be obtained from the efficient operation of an employment policy:

Staff of the CSO in 1945.

CENTRAL STATISTICAL OFFICE

52. **Mr. Spearman** asked the Chancellor of the Exchequer what is the present organisation of the Central Statistical Office.

Mr. Dalton: I will, with the hon. Member's permission, circulate this information in the OFFICIAL REPORT.

Following is the information:

CENTRAL STATISTICAL OFFICE.

Statisticians.

Director	1	Mr. H. Campion		£1,450 (fixed)
Chief Assistants	4	Mr. J. Stafford		£1,000
(£800–£1,000)		Mr. R. F. Fowler		£900
		Mr. R. H. Coarse		£850
		Mr. W. C. Taplin		£850
Assistants	6	Mr. B. N. Davies		£700
(£600–£800 men)		Mr. E. F. Jackson		£700
(£480–£775 women)		Mr. J. Cohen		£700
		Mr. C. R. Jones		£650
		Mr. R. E. Beales		£650
		Miss J. G. Marley		£530
Junior Assistants	7	Mr. L. T. Clarke		£450 + £50 allce.
(£260–£450 men)		Mr. T. Eastwood		£310
(£260–£425 women)		Mr. C. J. Martin		£450 + £100 ,,
		Mrs. E. J. Donovan		£400
		Miss M. O. Hardy		£310
		Miss P. M. Nye		£385
		Miss D. R. Shanahan		£425

Executive and Subordinate Staff.

Staff Officer	1	£550–£650
Chartists (women)	2	£200–£360
Clerical Officers (women)	10	£85–£280
Temporary Clerks (women) (Grade I)	1	62/6–76/6
,, ,, ,, (Grade II)	2	33/—66/6
,, ,, ,, (Grade III)	1	16/—59/-
Superintendent of Typists	1	£85–£280
Temporary Shorthand Typist, Grade I	2	40/—64/6
Established Typist	1	31/—60/-
Temporary Typists	6	25/—57/6
Established Messenger	1	£160–£205
Unestablished Messengers	4	56/6–58/6

(a) Statistics of employment and unemployment, including quarterly or monthly statements of present and prospective employment in the main industries and areas in the country, based on returns from employers.

(b) Regular information relating to savings, projected capital expenditure by public authorities, and, as far as possible, by private industry.

(c) An annual census of production showing the structure of the main groups of industries in the preceding year, including, inter alia, details of the quantity and value of output, stocks, and work in progress.

(d) Monthly figures of production, consumption and stocks, and, if possible, figures of orders on hand, based on sample returns obtained periodically throughout the year from large firms, trade associations, and public institutions.

(e) Annual and quarterly estimates of foreign capital movements and balance of foreign payments.

It is also proposed to develop the annual White Paper on National Income and Expenditure by providing a much more complete analysis than has hitherto been possible of the constituent parts of the country's total expenditure. In particular, direct estimates will be made of the various types of capital expenditure and the various sources of savings. This will be, in effect, the Capital Budget of the nation's wealth.'

Statistics of Trade Act, 1947.

10 & 11 GEO. 6.   CH. 39.

ARRANGEMENT OF SECTIONS.

Section.
1. Power of competent authorities to obtain information.
2. Census of production, distribution and services.
3. Returns for the purposes of census.
4. Offences relating to returns.
5. Power to prescribe additional subjects of inquiry by Order in Council.
6. Duty to notify undertakings to Board of Trade or other competent authority.
7. Report to Parliament.
8. Advisory committees.
9. Disclosure of information.
10. Information from persons entering or leaving the United Kingdom by air.
11. Orders.
12. Notices.
13. Offences by bodies corporate.
14. Power to require information about estimated cost of buildings.
15. Expenses.
16. Exercise of powers by Board of Trade.
17. Interpretation.
18. Application to Scotland.
19. Short title, extent and repeal.
    Schedule.

In 1945, the incoming Labour Prime Minister, Clement Attlee, set up a committee to oversee economic planning. This group, formally a sub-committee of the Lord President's Committee, comprised the Lord President (Herbert Morrison), the Chancellor of the Exchequer (Hugh Dalton), the president of the Board of Trade (Sir Stafford Cripps), and the Minister of Labour and National Service (George Isaacs).

Reporting to this group was a steering committee of senior officials under the chairmanship of Sir Edward Bridges. This committee organised its work through five working parties. The Statistical Working Party, chaired by Harry Campion, had by November 1945 completed a report on the permanent body of statistics required for employment policy. This report fixed the responsibility for collecting the different classes of statistics on to specified

Departments, and showed that additional legislative authority would be required to collect certain statistics.

Meanwhile, the Economic Survey Working Party, under the chairmanship of James Meade, had the task of reviewing the estimates and forecasts of national income and expenditure produced by the CSO and the Economic Section. It also produced a short term plan for 1946 based on these forecasts and the demands on economic resources implied by Departmental plans.

In the words of a contemporary document, the objectives were:

'To make sure that under post-war conditions the export trade, the re-equipment of industry, the housing programme and other essential civilian needs get their proper share of available resources. To consider the timing of major projects and other measures which may be necessary in order to implement the full employment policy.

To bring together into a coherent whole the work done by the many Departments responsible for individual projects of economic development or for particular aspects of the development (finance, manpower, building capacity, foreign exchange,

Jack Stafford (left) and C T Saunders at a Conference of European Statisticians in Geneva in the early 1950s.

The first *Monthly Digest of Statistics*.

UNITED KINGDOM

CENTRAL STATISTICAL OFFICE

MONTHLY DIGEST
OF
STATISTICS

No. 1
JANUARY 1946

LONDON: HIS MAJESTY'S STATIONERY OFFICE
PRICE 2s. 6d. NET

savings and so forth) without interfering with the responsibilities of the Departments concerned.'

The statistical programme set out in the CSO's plan was to form the basis of the Statistics of Trade Act, 1947. But before the bill was put before Parliament, further consultation was undertaken by means of two committees set up by the president of the Board of Trade; the Census of Production Committee (the 'Nelson Committee') and the Census of Distribution Committee (the 'Hopkins Committee'). These were set up in June 1945 by the Coalition President, Oliver Lyttleton, and reported to the Labour President, Sir Stafford Cripps. The committees comprised representatives of government statisticians (Campion, Leak, Meade), the industries concerned, and trade unionists.

Reactions to the bill were mixed. Representatives of industry, at a consultation meeting with officials, welcomed the information that the statistics would provide, but were less enthusiastic about filling in the forms. They were concerned about the impact on small firms, and the avoidance of duplication.

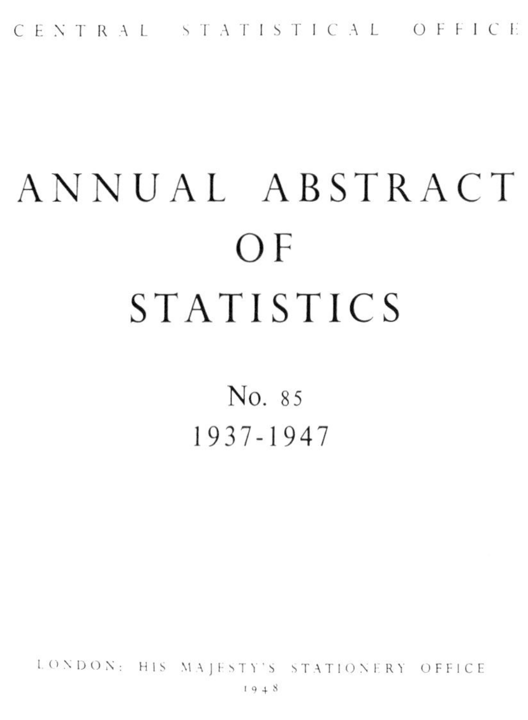

CENTRAL STATISTICAL OFFICE

ANNUAL ABSTRACT
OF
STATISTICS

No. 85

1937-1947

LONDON: HIS MAJESTY'S STATIONERY OFFICE
1948

ECONOMIC TRENDS

No. 1 NOVEMBER 1953

PUBLISHED FOR THE CENTRAL STATISTICAL OFFICE
BY H. M. STATIONERY OFFICE   PRICE 2s. 0d. NET

Members of Parliament were worried about practical difficulties and expressed concern about the constitutional implications. Some thought the powers of compulsion under the bill were too widely drawn, and could be used tyrannically. Others were concerned that the ability to disclose the contents of individual returns to other Departments was open to abuse. Understandable as these fears might have been, in the event they proved groundless.

The Statistics of Trade Act was passed in 1947. In addition to the programme of statistical development set out in the employment White Paper, the new Act provided for a census of distribution to be carried out for such years as the president of the Board of Trade should determine. This census was needed to fill a gap in the statistics of national output. The Act was the spur to development of economic statistics on a wide front.

Whilst work on the Statistics of Trade Act was in progress, other parts of the CSO were involved in forecasting work. In 1946 work started on an economic survey for 1950. This was to plan the direction in which the economy should change. A small team of economists and statisticians was formed to prepare the survey of the state of the economy in 1950. The planning team included Ronald Tress and Austin Robinson from the Economic Section and Christopher Saunders and Jack Stafford from the CSO.

Forecasting was a natural task for the CSO given that the Office was developing a comprehensive system of national accounts. The CSO and the Economic Section were equal partners in the National Income Forecast Working Party. From 1950 this took responsibility for the forecast of national income and expenditure. Christopher Saunders from the CSO became its first chairman. Other members of the working party were E F Jackson from the CSO and the economists Dow, Downie and Mrs Hemmings. Christopher Saunders, chief statistician, was also chairman of the World Economic Prospects Working Party which was set up in December 1953 with the aim to produce regular analyses of the world economic situation. In 1954 Christopher Saunders was made deputy director of the CSO. In the following year he was responsible for compiling *The National Accounts: Sources and Methods* which was published in 1956.

Other statisticians who played an important role in the development of economic statistics in the 1950s included Toby Paine, Philip Redfern, Leonard Nicholson, David Burdett, David Locke and Geoff Penrice. We now take a look at the origins of some of the CSO's familiar products, which first saw the light of day in Harry Campion's era.

Publications

Perhaps the first development to strike the public eye was the issue in January 1946 of the first *Monthly Digest of Statistics*. This was a published version of the Series B Digest circulated internally throughout the war. Its contents are shown in the Annex. The publication was welcomed widely, particularly by Members of Parliament who saw it as giving them the opportunity to make an informed contribution to the economic debate of the day. It is impossible to read the Hansard reports of the 1946 Budget debate, and the Supply Day debate on economic affairs later that year without being impressed by the high statistical content of the speeches. The price of a copy of the *Monthly Digest* was a mere half-crown ($12^1/_2$p in today's currency).

The first post-war *Annual Abstract* (which was also the first to be produced by the CSO) was published at the beginning of 1948.

Economic Trends, which took its name from a phrase in the introduction to the Statistics of Trade Act, did not appear until November 1953. It cost two shillings (10p).

Standard Industrial Classification (SIC)

Before the first SIC was introduced each Department devised its own classification of industry. There were three Departments principally involved, the Board of Trade (for censuses of production and other industrial statistics), the Ministry of Labour and National Service (employment statistics), and the Registrar-General's Department (censuses of population). The CSO brought the three Departments together in 1945 with Harry Campion in the chair to devise a common classification. Reg Beales, later to become deputy director of the CSO and a world expert on the national accounts, was secretary to the group.

Some of the headings in the old classifications are redolent of the age in which they were created. For example:

Accumulator battery maker

Bedstead maker, iron

Bedstead maker, brass

Clog maker

Driver, steam wagon, traction engine

Flower gatherer

Pea picker

Tripe dresser, cleaner.

The committee set itself three objectives:

(i) To adopt a common list of industry headings.

(ii) To agree common definitions for those headings.

(iii) To secure common groupings of the industries for summary purposes.

An early suggestion was that the new classification should be based on the pre-war League of Nations classification, in the design of which Sir Alfred Flux had been involved. However, this would have involved too much discontinuity with the past for all three Departments.

The approach adopted was to list the classifications used by the three Departments and note the difference between them. The committee then worked through the list, item by item, and hammered out an agreed coverage. In doing this they had an eye to the League of Nations classification, but found that in some respects it was unsuitable for the British industrial system. By this process agreement was reached on a three-digit classification consisting of 25 orders, 160 minimum list headings (so called because Departments agreed that all data would be collected at least to this level of detail), and 364 subdivisions.

The achievement of this measure of standardisation should not be underestimated. To make a change in a classification is troublesome and expensive. To introduce a discontinuity into a Department's statistics is unhelpful in the short term. To move away from a classification which was custom-built for a Department might have seemed a permanently retrograde step. It is to the credit of those involved that they took the broad view, and saw the powerful advantages of comparability between the statistics of different Departments.

After two years of painstaking work and negotiation, the SIC was complete in early 1947, and all that remained was to formally submit it to the Prime Minister. Imagine the consternation when the Cabinet Secretary replied to Jack Stafford that the Prime Minister would like Order 24 – Entertainment and Sport – broken down into two: 24a Entertainment and 24b Sport. Stafford responded that this had been considered but there were practical problems – the Royal Albert Hall, for example, was used for both entertainment and sport. The Prime Minister was unmoveable. He had given an undertaking in the House to Sir Alan Herbert, the composer Member of Parliament, that entertainment would be separately identifiable in statistics in future.

Index of industrial production

During the war a vast number of detailed statistics had been collected of the production of individual commodities. The Bridges Committee decided that to make this information meaningful a summary measure was needed. The Board of Trade had from 1928 to the outbreak of war produced a quarterly index of industrial production, based mainly on information collected voluntarily by trade associations and other organisations. This had been estimated to cover 70 per cent of the whole manufacturing and mining activity of the United Kingdom. However, in the course of wartime reorganisation the Board of Trade had lost responsibility for several key industries. The Central Statistical Office was therefore commissioned in 1947 to produce an index of industrial production. Economic conditions were changing fast. A quarterly index was no longer sufficient, so a monthly series was decided upon.

In the CSO a team of three, Tom Ridley, Joan Cox and Leonard Nicholson, were deputed to work up the index. Each was responsible for a group of SIC orders. Nearly 400 production series were used, mostly in the form of measures of physical production (eg tons of coal), rather than the deflated values preferred today.

They faced one big problem in determining weights. In principle these needed to be proportional to the net output of each industry –

Sir Norman Brook (later Lord Normanbrook).

BRADSHAW, THE WORLD'S MOST FAMOUS RAILWAY GUIDE, CEASES PUBLICATION SHORTLY.

"WE ARE ALWAYS AS IT WERE LOOKING UP A TRAIN IN LAST YEAR'S BRADSHAW"

— MR MACMILLAN, IN HIS BUDGET SPEECH, APRIL 17, 1956.

Cartoon in the *Evening Standard*, 1960

the value of output less purchases from other industries. This was information that could only be derived from a census of production. The passage of the Statistics of Trade Act in 1947 authorised annual censuses. However the earliest that one could be carried out was in respect of 1948 and results would not be available until 1949. The previous census had been in 1935, but the structure of industry had changed radically during the war.

The CSO team therefore produced an interim index using weights calculated from net output in 1935 from the census; from estimates of the net output of small firms not covered by the census; and from estimates of changes in the total wage bill of each industry between 1935 and 1946 obtained from the numbers of insured persons employed and average weekly earnings.

It had been intended to publish the index for the first time in March 1948, when two complete years' results would have been available for comparison. In January it was realised that the London and Cambridge Economic Service was about to publish its own index based on many of the same indicators. (It would have lacked the munitions production statistics, which were still secret. In 1948 the transfer of industries from munitions to civilian work was still proceeding, so this would have been a significant deficiency.) Sir Norman Brook put a submission to the Chancellor, Sir Stafford Cripps, proposing immediate publication. In answer to an arranged Parliamentary Question in early February 1948, the birth of the index of industrial production was announced.

Since that time the index has gone through eight rebasings and two more versions of the Standard Industrial Classification. It still covers broadly the same industries: mining, manufacturing, gas, electricity, water. It is still a base weighted arithmetic mean of its component indices. The index is important, not only in its own right, but also as the major component of the output measure of gross domestic product, which was first published in 1966.

The national accounts
The development of the national accounts in the early years was one of using the improvements stemming from the *Employment Policy White Paper* to put the annual accounts onto a firmer basis, to refine the understanding of the concepts involved and to provide more detailed analysis of the main aggregates. The 1946 White Paper

C T Saunders, with one of the early Blue Books.

(which sold for 9d – just under 4p!) comprised 50 quarto pages containing 27 tables and numerous notes. The content of the White Paper was expanded year by year until 1952, when the first *National Income and Expenditure Blue Book* was produced in September. The pre-Budget White Paper was then cut back to summary tables. Publishing the *Blue Book* in September enabled the CSO to produce many more tables (38 in total). The introduction of the *Blue Book* was followed by the publication in 1956 of the first edition of *Sources and Methods* which documented, for the benefit of users and compilers, the derivation of the figures and the principles of the system.

The next major development in the national accounts field was the start of work on quarterly accounts, part of a general move to improve short term statistics. This was publicly heralded in the 1956 Budget speech of the Chancellor of the Exchequer, Harold Macmillan, in which he made a comment which was to become notorious among government statisticians. He said: 'I am told that some of our statistics are too late to be as useful as they ought to be. We are always, as it were, looking up a train in last year's Bradshaw.' Later in the speech he returned to the subject, saying: 'I am still conscious of a certain gap in our defences in this matter and the need to strengthen our technical and administrative armoury. We must continually improve our statistics in form and timing.'

Then on 1 August 1956 the Chancellor made a further detailed statement on the need for improved statistics. He outlined seven ways in which the existing information could be improved. The first was a plea for industry to

Harold Macmillan, later Lord Stockton.

provide returns more quickly. The second was to increase the frequency with which certain statistics were collected. The remainder were proposals for specific areas of the accounts:

Fixed investment and stocks in the distributive and service trades.
Building and civil engineering contracts.
Quarterly estimates of company profits.
Balance of payments capital account.
Households income and expenditure, a continuous survey.

The Chancellor's speech concluded:

'We are considering what improvements and extensions can be made in the presentation and publication of statistics so that Parliament, industry and the public may be kept as well informed as possible. One important objective is to combine the available information into quarterly estimates of national expenditure and its components, similar to the annual figures given in the National Income Blue Book and Economic Surveys.'

The CSO had been producing quarterly estimates of consumers' expenditure for several years, but to produce full quarterly national accounts required the collaboration of other Departments to produce the new quarterly inquiries into fixed investment, stocks and company profits, announced by the Chancellor. Although some of these inquiries had been introduced before the speech, it was an effective way to announce all the improvements, and to seek the support of respondents.

The first quarterly figures of national expenditure were published in 1957, followed by quarterly factor income estimates in the following year. Constant price estimates appeared in 1959. By 1960 there were long enough series to calculate seasonally adjusted estimates.

Balance of payments

The 1944 *Employment Policy White Paper* had on its statistical shopping list, 'annual and quarterly estimates of foreign capital movements and balance of foreign payments'. By the time Macmillan made his speech in 1956 there were annual and half-yearly estimates, but still no quarterly figures. Of the seven proposals for improvement listed in the speech, that which related to the balance of payments was the least concrete: 'We are studying, in co-operation with the Bank of England, how we can best improve the statistics of the balance of payments, especially capital transactions.'

In the 1950s the balance of payments statistics were the responsibility of the Bank of England, which compiled them primarily from visible trade statistics produced by the Board of Trade and from data arising from the operation of exchange control. With the gradual relaxation of exchange control the quality of the estimates suffered, and it became necessary to substitute data based on direct inquiries, mainly conducted by government Departments. Such a system was very similar to that of the national accounts, with which there were links. In 1960 responsibility for the balance of payments was transferred to the CSO, although the Bank of England continued to supply an important part of the data.

FINANCIAL STATISTICS

CENTRAL STATISTICAL OFFICE

No.3   JULY   1962

LONDON: HER MAJESTY'S STATIONERY OFFICE
Price 7s. 6d. net.

The first annual balance of payments statistics were published in a pre-Budget White Paper in 1948 (Command 7324). It consisted of six pages with three tables – current account, capital account and drain on reserves. In 1960, with the transfer came the first publication of quarterly statistics, and the first *Balance of Payments Pink Book*.

Financial statistics

In the mid 1950s the government had been operating a combination of fiscal and monetary policies with variable success. It was decided to set up a committee to look into the working of the monetary system, chaired by Lord Radcliffe, a Law Lord of immense experience in public inquiries of all kinds. Geoff Penrice was secretary to the committee. Peter Thorneycroft, the Chancellor of the Exchequer, described the system as it then operated as resembling 'an antiquated pumping machine, creaking and groaning, leaking wildly at all the main valves, but still desperately attempting to keep down the level of water in the mine'. The committee was asked to examine the old machine, advise generally on its limitations, and recommend whether it should be patched up or replaced by something better.

The CSO with the co-operation of the Treasury and the Bank of England produced three papers for the committee, bringing together the statistics that were available. These proved to be quite patchy. At the end of its deliberations, among other recommendations, the committee called for a considerable extension to the collection of financial statistics. A system of financial accounts for the sectors of the economy was drawn up by the CSO's Laurie Berman in conjunction with the Bank of England, the Treasury and the Board of Trade. Standard definitions and classifications were agreed, and arrangements for collecting both stocks and transactions in financial instruments were devised and negotiated with the main financial institutions – banks, building societies, insurance companies, pension funds and so on, and public sector institutions. As they became available, the results were incorporated into the financial accounts and were published, along with other financial information – interest rates, exchange rates – in the publication *Financial Statistics*, which first appeared in 1962.

The Estimates Committee

Towards the end of 1965 the Estimates Committee of the House of Commons decided that its sub-committee on Economic Affairs should examine the Government Statistical Service. During the first six months of 1966 the sub-committee took written and oral evidence from the CSO, other Departments and from outside bodies and individuals using or contributing to official statistics. The sub-committee's report was published later in the year and made 23 specific recommendations, over half of which referred to the CSO. Most of these were directed to enhancing the status and co-ordinating role of the CSO. Examples were that the CSO should make an immediate examination of the forms used by Departments with a view to increased standardisation; the CSO should take the lead in developing the use of computers for statistical purposes; it should co-ordinate the use of registers and classifications; and should co-ordinate the development of publications throughout the Government Statistical Service.

The recommendations in the report were accepted by the government with only minor qualifications and from early 1967 steps were taken to implement them. It was necessary to recruit additional staff – professional, executive and clerical – and to restructure the office at a time when the government was imposing overall constraints on the size of the Civil Service. In March 1967 Sir Harry Campion retired, and the implementation of the committee's recommendations was left to his successor, Professor C A Moser.

CHAPTER VI

THE MOSER
YEARS

Sir Claus Moser.

Claus Moser joined the Central Statistical Office in April 1967 soon after the Estimates Committee report on the Government Statistical Service had put forward a number of specific recommendations. The central theme of the Estimates Committee report was that the increasing demands on the Government Statistical Service, and their complexity, required a much greater degree of central management by the CSO. This was felt to be a prerequisite for producing better and more efficient statistics.

Claus Moser joined the Central Statistical Office from the London School of Economics, where he was professor of social statistics. Professor Moser studied at the London School of Economics from 1940 to 1943, where he obtained a degree in statistics. After service in the Royal Air Force from 1943 to 1946 he returned to the LSE, where he was made an assistant lecturer and subsequently lecturer in statistics. In 1955 he became a reader in social statistics and was appointed professor in 1961. Professor Moser had published a number of works on statistical techniques and their application in the social field. He was a fellow of the British Academy and from 1961 to 1963 was statistical adviser to the Robbins Committee on Higher Education.

Harold Wilson was Prime Minister when Professor Moser took up the reins of the CSO. He recalls having a series of meetings with Claus Moser and Sir Burke Trend, secretary to the Cabinet. Moser produced a document setting out a programme of reforms that went much wider than the recommendations in the Estimates Committee. The report was considered by Harold Wilson to be a charter for statistical reform because it led to better statistics both for the use of government and for industrial decision-making, as well as providing a basis for academic analyses and public comment. The report was presented to a new Cabinet committee set up by Harold Wilson consisting, unusually, of specially selected, numerate junior ministers and officials, including the Departmental statisticians. Its chairman was first Peter Shore, a numerate economist, and then Edmund Dell, a statistically trained ICI industrial planner. The committee was serviced by the Cabinet Office and the CSO jointly. Harold Wilson chaired the first meeting and he recalled that he found it over-cautious. Wilson detected a lack of enthusiasm on the part of some permanent secretaries, perhaps on empire building or empire retention grounds. Harold Wilson also noted that his suspicions did not extend to the Departmental statisticians who naturally were supportive of the direction of the reforms which were being sought.

Harold Wilson indicated some of the background to the consideration of Claus Moser's report in his presidential address to the Royal Statistical Society in 1972. Before the war Harold Wilson had been head of the Manpower Statistics Branch at the Ministry of Labour, where he worked with Mr A Reader and Sir William Beveridge. In 1941 he took over the Mines Department statistical division. During the next two years a system was introduced under which nearly every ton of coal consumed, by type of consumer and by significant customer, could be accounted for. The use of coal during the war was an intensely political issue. With this background of working on government statistics

the recollection of Claus Moser's early years by Harold Wilson are of interest. He said:

'The committee, by its composition of junior ministers and senior civil servants, represented a departure from the more usual committee structure. The Prime Minister attached great importance to the work of the committee and hoped it would liberally interpret its terms of reference by not only keeping the existing situation regarding statistics under review but also carrying through a fundamental revolution in government statistics, particularly in the industrial and financial fields. Whilst the committee would no doubt be producing a number of general reports it would be important for them to note from time to time the changes which were being made. Our existing statistics were held in high regard in many quarters but they were seriously deficient in a number of respects and often failed to provide the necessary information on which to base operational planning and to take policy decisions at the appropriate time.

In the case of financial statistics, the figures for the balance of payments appeared three months after the end of the period to which they related. This meant that it was possible that decisions had to be taken in fundamental areas of policy in the absence of the relevant statistics. To bring about some improvement in the situation, the voluntary co-operation of the various organisations concerned should be sought in obtaining the necessary data much more quickly – especially figures in respect of invisibles. The Lord Mayor of London was closely associated with this particular area of activity and his help was to be sought.

Another major problem related to the index of production. The index was not accurate to within a margin of two points and the figures were constantly in need of revision. The Prime Minister understood that the index was based up to 50 per cent on figures which were six months old and on the rest on samples and estimates. It was important that the index for a particular month should be based on figures related to that period. The index of production was basic to economic forecasting and also to a proper assessment of past performance. The prevailing situation led both to problems on forecasting and *to difficulties regarding policy decisions as between individual Departmental interests. The task of improving the index of production both in quality and in its timing would constitute a high priority in the work of the committee. Figures for investment were critical as one of the determinants of the economy. Decisions regarding economic stimuli, reflation and investment had been taken on the basis of investment statistics which were substantially revised. Forecasts based on the subjective view of industrial companies regarding investment were at the centre of economic planning.'*

After a brief reference to the need for improving regional statistics the Prime Minister, according to the record of the first meeting of the Statistical Committee, went on:

'The present basis of collection of statistics involved a diversity of sources – some good but extremely slow, such as the Census of Production. There was scope for rationalisation on the basis of a single monthly return by a firm covering all information required by government. The data sought would cover the various Departmental interests, eg particulars of employment, value added, material usage, fuel inputs, etc, which could be computerised to produce information about production, labour utilisation and the investment situation within two to three weeks after the end of the period to which the information related. Figures for the private housing sector were particularly in need of improvement – especially having regard to their implication for social planning. Evidence of what could be done on the basis of rapidly collecting

good material was shown in the production of such indices as the cost of living index and figures regarding unemployment.

What was the place of the Central Statistical Office in the government machine? The problem was not to consider the location of the CSO in the government organisation but its role and the material made available to it. Industrial statistics constituted the biggest problem and action was required by the industrial Departments to enable the CSO to carry out its minimal task more easily and also to enable it to assume a more positive role in encouraging Departments and advising them regarding methods and techniques. Departments needed to be told what questions required to be answered.

Manpower was fundamental to the whole problem. The committee might well consider it advisable to set up a sub-committee to look into the supply of statisticians for the government service and their training. This would probably need to be done at an early stage in their deliberations since if their conclusions led to a requirement for substantial additional manpower it would be prudent for the possibility of securing them to have already been considered. The conditions of service of government statisticians will need to be examined together with the possibility of recruiting statisticians from industry on say a two or three year secondment. An arrangement of this kind would be productive both to the government and also to industry.'

Claus Moser's programme was endorsed. The Prime Minister informed the committee of his intention to take the chair at intervals, particularly when there was inter-departmental disagreement or major decisions had to be taken – in other words when Claus Moser and his fellow statisticians needed backing. It was further laid down that all recommendations of the committee requiring a decision would be put in the form of a minute by its chairman to the Prime Minister and to be given effect by a Downing Street directive.

Moser's set of proposals was spelled out in a 50-page memorandum. This was the blueprint of the wide-ranging reforms which took place in the late 1960s and early 1970s. The measures introduced became widely known, as he took pains to explain what he was doing to all potential users in industry, Parliament, press and the social services.

Moser realised that a centralised Statistical Office facilitated the efficient production of statistics but in terms of their efficient utilisation within government, he saw the weight of advantage lying with a decentralised system. Because of this dilemma, particular attention was paid in the development of the CSO to its role in co-ordinating the statistical activities of individual Departments. A central theme of Moser's proposal was that the increasing demands on the Government Statistical Service, and their complexity, required a much greater degree of central management by the CSO. This he felt to be a prerequisite for producing better and more efficient statistics. After a year as director of the CSO Moser put forward proposals, early in 1968, for a reorganisation aimed at giving the CSO an increased role in managing statistics across Departments. These proposals were accepted and in 1968 Moser became head of the Government Statistical Service.

Another proposal, aiming to combine the advantages of the centralised and decentralised arrangements, was the setting up of two major agencies – the Business Statistics Office and the Office of Population, Censuses and Surveys – and the establishment at the CSO of four units which together provided a system of central management services for the Government Statistical Service.

The Business Statistics Office (BSO) came into being at the beginning of 1969 under the direction of Martin Fessey. Its programme of work was to take on most of the government's collection of statistics from businesses, irrespective of the Department requiring the information. It was envisaged that it would take over inquiries for the Department of Trade and Industry, Department of Employment, Department of the Environment and the Ministry of Agriculture, Fisheries and Food. By centralising inquiries it was considered that communication with industry would be improved and it would be easier to co-ordinate and integrate different inquiries. The Office was developed out of the Board of Trade Census Office at Eastcote and remained, for daily management, part of the Department of Trade and Industry. It was, however, closely linked to the CSO, partly through a management committee of which Claus Moser was the chairman. Premises, tailor-made for the BSO, were built at Newport in Monmouthshire.

The Office of Population, Censuses and Surveys (OPCS) was established in 1970 through a merger of the General Register Office and the Government Social Survey. Its director was Michael Reed who also was the registrar-general for England and Wales. The Office was to be responsible for most of the collection of statistical information from persons and households through its programme of censuses, surveys and registration. It was to carry out the continuous surveys used by a number of Departments – the family expenditure survey and a new general household survey. It retained the responsibilities of its two original component bodies. OPCS was a separate Department, but again with close links to the CSO, including a policy committee under Moser's chairmanship.

The four new CSO units which carried out much of the central management services for the Government Statistical Services were:

Computer and Data Systems Unit
This unit had the general responsibility in conjunction with the Management Services Division of the Civil Service Department, for planning computer developments of government statistics and was involved in planning the computer configurations for the BSO and OPCS. The unit also handled computer facilities for the CSO.

Statistical Standards and Classification Unit
This unit had the task of securing as much uniformity as possible, in the use of definitions, concepts and classifications by different Departments.

Survey Control Unit
Survey Control was concerned with keeping a critical watch on all official demands for statistical information. The work of the new unit was to examine all new and existing inquiries. The aim was to eliminate unnecessary statistical surveys, to reduce the burdens of others and generally to ensure that demands on suppliers of statistics were coherent, orderly and kept to a minimum.

Programme Development Unit
The task of this unit was to draw together the plans and programmes of Departmental statistics divisions to establish priorities and to ensure the best use of resources. Statistical programmes and priorities within policy Departments reflect the relative importance of the tasks and policies which the statistics are designed to service. The unit's work was nevertheless important in trying to produce out of these individual tasks a co-ordinated and integrated scheme for the development of Government statistics as a whole. The unit was closely linked with Claus Moser's overall management duties as head of the Government Statistical Service.

When Claus Moser came to office in 1967, Reg Beales was deputy director. In addition the CSO was managed by a senior team of six chief statisticians – Leonard Nicholson, Bill Stedman-Jones, Harold Bishop, Laurie Berman, John Walton and Rita Maurice. The ambitious programme which Claus was following necessitated a restructuring of the Office. By mid-1969, three new Grade 3 (under secretary) posts were created. These were filled by Tom Pilling, Laurie Berman and Harold Bishop. In 1969 the number of chief statistician/assistant secretary posts had expanded to nine. Stanley James, Ron Green, John Harding, David Harris, Sydney Rosenbaum and Robert Brown were appointed to the CSO alongside John Walton,

Harold Bishop and Laurie Berman.

Rita Maurice and Bill Stedman-Jones. In 1970, on Harold Bishop's death, Stanley James was promoted. He in turn was replaced by Alec Sorrell as chief statistician.

One of the major areas for improvement in Moser's first few years was social statistics. Indeed when Harold Wilson appointed Moser, he particularly asked that social statistics be given greater priority. At that time about 40 per cent of professional statisticians in the Government were working on social statistics. However, there were some problems. Historically, social statistics emerged in a fragmented way as by-products of administrative processes in education, law, population, registration, and so on. They therefore were related to particular areas of administration rather than to particular population groups. The fragmentation of social statistics was reflected in the CSO being involved in this area in only a minor way. However with moves towards more integrated thinking about social policies, towards development of systems of social statistics and towards greater use of multi-purpose surveys, the CSO became more involved. In the late 1960s there was a strong social statistics division in the CSO which had close relations with the Office of Population, Censuses and Surveys.

The first visible result to come out of the social statistics division was the publication of *Social Trends* in 1970. This statistical volume was perhaps above all a symbol of the CSO's new attitude towards social statistics – a bringing together of the parts of the jigsaw puzzle so that information about different aspects of social life was increasingly connected. Various other projects started to help in the same direction. The family expenditure survey was strengthened and expanded in coverage. A continuous general household survey which contained a regular core of questions relating to the output of social policies was introduced. Ron Fry was the chief statistician involved in this work. A second chief statistician post in social statistics was created at the CSO in 1971 and filled by Muriel Nissel on promotion.

In 1971 John Boreham moved from the Ministry of Technology to the Central Statistical Office as an assistant director. At the same time the deputy director Reg Beales was upgraded to deputy secretary. A year later Reg Beales retired as deputy director. Beales entered the

First edition of *Social Trends*.

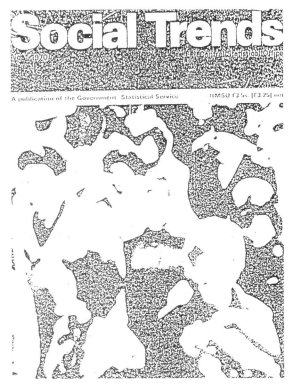

72

Government Statistical Service in 1943 as a senior executive officer. He originally trained as an actuary working first with Norwich Union and then the Northern Life Assurance Company. His first work in the CSO was involved with the development of the Standard Industrial Classification and with CSO's publications. He launched the *Monthly Digest of Statistics*. He was promoted to statistician in 1949 and later that year moved to the Board of Inland Revenue as its chief statistician. Beales returned to the CSO in 1957 as deputy director and had responsibility for developing the national accounts. On his retirement, after 15 years as deputy director, he was replaced by John Boreham on promotion.

At this time there was a major move of senior staff in the Office. Laurie Berman moved to the Department of Trade and Industry to replace Jack Stafford who had retired after 24 years. A new under secretary post was created. The four assistant directors in 1972 were John Walton, Alex Sorrell, Stanley James and Owen Nankivell. It was in this year that the number of chief statistician posts increased to 14. In October of that year the chief statisticians in post were Jack Hibbert, Ron Green, Roger Norton, Geoff Dean, Sydney Rosenbaum, David Harris, Barry Wakefield, John Harding, Ron Fry, and Muriel Nissel. The vacancies which existed at that time were subsequently filled by Peter Stibbard, Peter Kenny, and Brian Mower. In 1973 Claus Moser was knighted.

The expansion which had occurred in the early 1970s in part reflected the need of the statistical system to be flexible and cope with changing policy requirements. Examples of the changes that were required reflected the high rate

Sir Claus Moser at an international conference with Ron Fry opposite and Rosemary Medlar to his left.

Laurie Berman.

Jack Stafford.

Ron Green and Owen Nankivell.

Mayer, Director-General of Eurostat in 1973.

of inflation which caused problems in using price indices as deflators. There were also statistical issues associated with North Sea Oil and with energy statistics which needed to be developed. The increased spotlight on the distribution of income and wealth had many statistical implications. There were also numerous statistical challenges expected to emanate from possible membership of the European Community.

Enlargement of the European Community was provided by the Paris Summit of October 1972. The Statistical Office of the European Community (SOEC) had around 200 staff of whom 40 per cent were equivalent to professional statisticians. The Office was located in Luxembourg and removed from the day-to-day policy making in the remainder of the Commission. At the head of the Office was a director-general, Mr J Mayer, equivalent in rank to the heads of the Directorates-General dealing with policy issues. Mr Mayer was responsible to a commissioner (R Dahrendorf).

In 1973 SOEC was organised into six divisions. These dealt with general statistics, energy statistics, trade and transport statistics, industrial statistics, social statistics and agricultural statistics. SOEC had made great strides in harmonising statistical data from the member states and in carrying out important statistical inquiries on a consistent basis in each member country. It was also being faced with a large increase in demand for statistical information and with trying to find better procedures for assessing and balancing priorities for statistical projects. An important element in this process was the twice-yearly meeting of the heads of National Statistical Offices of the

Community countries under the chairmanship of the director-general of SOEC to develop an agreed statistical programme looking several years ahead.

The SOEC work programme which was put together at the Conference of Heads of National Statistics Offices was carried out in detail mainly through *ad hoc* working groups under the chairmanship of SOEC. These identified the Community interest through multilateral groups of experts from member states. Membership of the EC imposed upon the United Kingdom the

need to provide statistical information covering the EC directives and regulations that were in force. Providing the required statistics and refocusing the development programme on to a European dimension was a major challenge for the Government Statistical Service. In 1973 the CSO saw the departure of David Harris, a chief statistician who moved to SOEC. At the same time, several statisticians from the Government Statistical Service moved to Luxembourg to fill vacancies that were created upon Britain's accession.

In 1974 Stanley James, Grade 3, moved to the Department of Trade and Industry. A year later Barry Wakefield was promoted to under-secretary following Tom Pilling's move to the Department of Trade and Industry.

In the early part of 1976, the government decided to adopt new procedures for arriving at an overall and integrated view of social policies,

Tom Pilling with Owen Nankivell in Moscow.

with special attention to the ways in which social policies interrelate and interact. The government had before it a report by the Central Policy Review Staff of the Cabinet Office (often called the Think Tank) on the need for 'A Joint Framework for Social Policies'. This proposed a coherent strategy for social objectives expressed in general terms (for example economic and social equality); objectives concerned with individual programmes (for example pensions); and objectives dealing with particular groups in society (the disabled, for example). The aim was to improve co-ordination between services as they affected the individual, with better analysis of policy prescriptions for major problems; especially those cutting across Departments. A new 'social group' was formed in the CSO to carry out the statistical work on this.

In 1977 there was another change of staff at under secretary level. This year saw the departure of John Walton to take over as director of statistics at Inland Revenue. He was replaced by Jack Hibbert on promotion. There was also a small reshuffle among the chief statisticians with Deo Ramprakash's name being added to that of Peter Kenny, Maurice Wilde, Tony Rushbrook, John Ludley, Geoff Dean, Peter Stibbard, Shirley Carter, Michael Lockyer, David Wroe, David Flaxen and Eric Thompson.

On 1 August 1978 Sir Claus resigned from the post as head of the Government Statistical Service and director of the CSO. This brought to an end 11 years of statistical development and reorganisation conducted under his inspiration and leadership. In 1978 the number of statistical staff at the CSO was 60, nearly three times the number when he started in 1967.

Edmund Dell the Secretary of State for Trade and chairman of the Statistical Policy Committee indicated that:

John Walton.

'his personal charm and flair was crucial. His ability to establish a warm rapport with people of all sorts, from the most junior members of his staff to senior officials and Ministers, including three Prime Ministers, was at the heart of his great success. Underlying all of this was his determination to see that statistics should be actively used for the benefit of the nation by way of social and economic policies. He worked hard to

ensure that decisions in central government, local government, industry and commerce were never impaired by any lack of timely, relevant and well presented statistics. He was just as concerned that Parliament and people should be provided with a service of accurate and comprehensible facts and figures as a basis for sensible discussion of current issues.'

Upon being asked what advice he would give to a successor, Sir Claus said:

'I would say, cut back a bit on collection. Analyse and interpret more. We are not figure collectors, we are statisticians. We are part of policy, part of the management of the nation and what could be more important? So do analysis and interpretation as far as the market will bear and above all never give in on an issue that you feel deep down is an integrity issue.'

On leaving Office, Sir Claus became a director of N M Rothschild and chairman of the Economist Intelligence Unit. Numerous other appointments followed in the 1980s. Beside statistics, music played an important part in his life. A talented musician himself, he was also chairman of the Royal Opera House between 1974 and 1987 and a member of the governing body of the Royal Academy of Music from 1969 to 1979. He became warden of Wadham College, Oxford in 1984 and was made chancellor of the University of Keele in 1986.

Deo Ramprakash.

Shirley Carter and Peter Kenny.

CHAPTER VII

THE BOREHAM
YEARS

Sir John Boreham.

John Boreham became director of the Central Statistical Office and head of the Government Statistical Service on 1 August 1978. He was educated at Marlborough and Trinity College, Oxford. When he arrived at Oxford after serving in the Royal Air Force, he recalled that he did not really know what he was going to do and chose the philosophy, politics and economics degree because it did not close many options. His tutor Tony Crosland advised him to concentrate on economics. He found he had to choose an optional subject. Boreham decided that statistics would be easy for him as he had done mathematics. When he was at Oxford he was married and had a son so he needed an option that was not too over-burdening. So he did statistics and found that it suited him very well.

Following a short spell at the Agricultural Economic Research Institute in Oxford, Boreham joined the statistics division of the Ministry of Food as a higher executive officer in 1950. It was in the following year that he took up an appointment as an assistant statistician with the Ministry of Agriculture. He transferred to the General Register Office in 1955. In 1958 he moved to the Central Statistical Office and five years later he returned to the General Register Office on promotion to chief statistician. He became director of economics and statistics at the Ministry of Technology from 1967 to 1971, and was appointed deputy director of the CSO in 1972.

It was reported in *The Times* in June 1978 that 'Sir Claus Moser's leaving present to Mr Boreham was a 40-page survey of his period in office and a blueprint for the next ten years'. We have hints at what was in this blueprint. Sir Claus was impressed by the French INSEE where statisticians are centralised but a number are posted out to Departments working in statistics divisions on special projects. There were also criticisms that the Business Statistics Office Management Committee was not effective, unlike the informal steering group overseeing work priorities at the Office of Population and Census Surveys. Another problem, reflecting the decentralised system, was the difficulty in setting priorities and formulating the Government Statistical Service's work programme. To get central control of the work programme would require a Ministerial policy committee to be set up to consider the programme.

No doubt John Boreham was considering these blueprints. As deputy director of the CSO since 1972 he would have been well aware of the thinking behind them. To implement them would have required a political direction. But this was not to be, as the tide started to turn in 1979. A new government came into office with new ideas about the role of government and the direction it was to take. The government announced its policy to reduce the size of the Civil Service – so the emphasis on the future had to change. A review of the CSO and the GSS became an early part of the government's programme.

On 21 January 1980, the Prime Minister, Margaret Thatcher, commissioned a review of the Government Statistical Service under Sir Derek Rayner. Its purpose was to examine critically the statistical services available to each Minister and the use made of them by:

(i) assessing each statistical activity to see whether the cost to government and those to outside were justified by the benefits obtained and whether the work could be undertaken more efficiently.

(ii) recommending the best means for the continuing scrutiny of the cost of, and the need for, individual statistical services.

Sir Derek Rayner composed a small team to undertake the review. Ian Beesley, chief statistician in Branch 11 in the CSO looking after social surveys was seconded to the review team. Richard Wilson from the Civil Service Department also became a member as did George Wise, who was on loan from Natwest Bank.

John Boreham, in a message to statisticians, said that the review had his strong personal backing and that he was going to take a close interest in its progress:

'I regard it as essential that the Government Statistical Service should have the full confidence of Ministers if we are to do a good job. This means we must be prepared to look at existing work with fresh eyes, to weed out that which is not necessary for government to do, to identify any gaps which are really worth filling, and to ensure that what we do is done to maximum effect.

The search for cost savings is important. I know that Sir Derek Rayner sets particular store by identifying that statistical work which is wholly necessary for central government and seeing it is first rate for the purpose.'

The objectives of the CSO had not changed very much under successive governments since they were considered in the Estimates Committee report in 1966. John Boreham described them as:

(i) To make sure that each Minister (especially the Prime Minister and the Chancellor of the Exchequer) has an adequate and cost-effective statistical service.

(ii) To make sure that the Cabinet need never argue about statistics.

(iii) To maintain the integrity of government statistics and to maintain public belief in that integrity.

(iv) To make sure that as far as possible Parliament and the public have a ready access to the same statistical information as is available to Ministers.

(v) To maintain liaison with the profession and participate in developing statistical techniques.

Laurie Berman, Roger Thatcher and John Boreham, enjoying an international conference.

(vi) To maintain the United Kingdom's contribution to international statistics.

The review team regarded these objectives as too open ended and in need of sharper emphasis on value for money. Their report was to make several practical suggestions designed to improve value for money. The cost of the CSO was about £3.75 million per year in 1980 and on the 1 July of that year the CSO had 61 professional statisticians and 173 other staff.

About half of the CSO's budget went on macro-economic data. These included the quarterly and annual system of national accounts which provided a framework for the analysis of economic developments relevant to both monetarist and Keynesian economics. The important outputs were the national accounts, financial flow statistics, the index of production, the balance of payments, estimates of income and redistribution, and the tax and price index.

A further 15 per cent of the budget was spent on services to government statistics of a head office type. The director, who as head of the Government Statistical Service was head of profession, sought to influence and to co-ordinate the work of statistical divisions in Departments in pursuit of his objectives to ensure common standards. Around 12 per cent of the CSO's budget was spent on social statistics – income distribution, social trends, and general briefing for Ministers on social subjects. The remainder of the CSO's budget was made up of computing and office services.

The review team noted that since 1965 CSO's expenditure had grown over $2^{1}/_{2}$ times in real terms. The extra expenditure since 1965 had

REVIEW OF
GOVERNMENT STATISTICAL SERVICES

Report to the
Prime Minister

by
Sir Derek Rayner

Price £2·90   December 1980

mainly gone on additional staff for social statistics, publications, press and information, GSS policy and co-ordination, and computing. There were corresponding increases in senior posts at under secretary level and above. However by the start of 1980/81 real costs were seven per cent lower than in 1975. Between the government taking office in May 1979 and May 1980 staff numbers were reduced by 11 per cent to 235.

The growth in expenditure since 1965 was questioned by the review team as to whether it was well founded. The review team commented that on the whole they thought any excesses were excesses of enthusiasm. The team commented that a highly numerate approach to the analysis of macro-economic policy issues had become part of central economic decision taking. However, in the expansion, the team regarded the statistical services provided by the CSO as not always subject to rigorous appraisal of value for money.

The team regarded the primary duty of the CSO was to service central government requirements. In doing so it had to ensure Ministers were advised what their requirements for statistics should be and Ministers should be advised directly where necessary. The team acknowledged that statistics could not be turned on and off like a tap. But the government was entitled to expect its statistical services to be responsive to its changing requirements and data should be cut out where they cease to give value for money. A main plank of the review team's thinking was that the CSO had not been aggressive enough in pursuit of value for money and elimination of waste.

The extra work since 1965 on social monitoring provided new statistical tools and assessments, for example, social trends, work and support of the Royal Commission on the distribution of income and wealth, and support of the joint framework for social policy. Almost all the work was justified by the policy needs at the time. The review team pointed out that these needs had changed and that it was right to expect the CSO to respond to the changes. The team found that the CSO was too heavily committed to serving the public at large. The expansion of the press, information and publications was intended to make government statistics as widely available as possible to give people the full facts of economic and social change and to maintain public confidence in the integrity of statistics. The team questioned whether value for money is

encouraged when the CSO was based on meeting regular demands for statistics through publications. They argued that it was difficult in such circum-stances to withdraw statistics or to put them on a care and maintenance basis. Statistical services, they claimed, became like a coral reef – continuing secretion and little erosion. The review team also had some praise for the CSO. They noted that the Treasury was well content with its output and they noted the widespread belief amongst the CSO's own staff in the importance of the majority of its statistics. The team noted that Ministers did not have to defend themselves against charges of cooking the national books. The statistical service's reputation for honesty and integrity was considered by the Rayner Team as an asset to government which it would be in the government's interest to protect. Also the feedback from outside users of the value of statistical publications was found to be favourable.

The team's recommendations were intended to shift the emphasis towards a closer CSO relationship with central government, requiring statisticians to provide interpretive assistance of the required quality – not just of the highest quality possible. Also to address specific questions in a down to earth and practical way. Finally, for the statistics to be both relevant and responsive. The recommendations sought the flexible use of talent and enhanced opportunity for the main working grades to stretch their wings.

The recommendations of the Rayner Review both of the CSO and of the statistics divisions of Departments were published in a government White Paper in April 1981. The review team proposed a reduction between May 1979 and April 1984 in the total cost of the CSO's budget in real terms of 33 per cent. Associated with this they proposed a reduction in manpower of 25 per cent from 263 in May 1979 to 196 in April 1984. The savings were to come from limiting work to that essential for government, ending the subsidy on editorial costs of CSO publications and restructuring the Office to save senior posts. Resources devoted to balance of payments statistics were to be reduced reflecting the change in the United Kingdom's overseas trading position. Benchmark analyses of economic transactions (input/output) were to continue to be produced every five years and to be updated for at most one intermediate year. The frequency of income distribution estimates was to be reduced and the CSO's work on wealth distribution stopped. The review recommended that the Survey Control Unit be strengthened and the existing regular business surveys throughout government Departments and Agencies be periodically reviewed.

For the Government Statistical Service as a whole Rayner planned to save £25 million a year representing about one quarter of the total staff and administrative costs. This meant shedding some 2,500 posts from the 9,000 civil servants providing statistical services.

John Boreham was knighted in 1980. Early the following year he sent a message to the statistician group:

'Eighteen months ago, we all feared that implementing the recommendations would involve great difficulties, perhaps including redundancies. It has been a great relief to me and to all of us that this has not happened. We are in sight of the full implementation of all the Rayner decisions and it is clear that no involuntary redundancies in the statistician group will take place.

This is partly because we had anticipated some of the necessary cuts, partly because the cuts affect professional staff less than the administration group, partly because we have been able to find alternative jobs for statisticians both inside the Civil Service and outside and partly because we have been able to offer early retirement to a small number of volunteers.

We have undergone a very detailed scrutiny of our work and have a broad confirmation of its value, plus an acceptance that to carry it out we need the professional staff numbers currently in post. The broad framework of statistics remains intact and we have an increased confidence in its value. The importance of statistical advice to Ministers has been reaffirmed and we now have a greater opportunity to make sure that what we provide is used in a most effective way.

This post-Rayner period is a challenge to our professionalism. Good management and new ideas, the use of new technology and new techniques, can make the GSS more efficient and more effective and add zest to many existing jobs. It is never wholly satisfying to work away, however well and with however great dedication, feeling that the output is academic or is ignored by those who should be benefiting from it. This should no longer be the case. Starting from our new base, with an imaginative and innovative attitude to our work and a clear view of the benefit to be derived from it, we can raise the reputation of the GSS even higher, both outside and inside the Service.'

Sir John Boreham had implemented many of the Rayner recommendations by mid-1981. In the CSO, Sir John took a hard look at the developments of the previous decade, studied their costs and benefits closely and made decisions about priorities. He achieved a good deal of streamlining and compression while still providing the same statistical service to government. He made big reductions in methodological research and in briefing on social policy. He reduced the frequency of income distribution statistics and input-output tables. All work on the distribution of wealth was stopped. By all these changes the CSO was reduced from 263 in May 1979 to under 200 by early 1982.

**GOVERNMENT
STATISTICAL
SERVICES**

*Presented to Parliament by the Lord President of the Council
by Command of Her Majesty
April 1981*

One of the recommendations of the Rayner Report was that Sir John should reduce the senior staff of the Office. When he took over in 1978, the deputy director post which he vacated was available and Jack Hibbert, Owen Nankivell, Barry Wakefield and Alec Sorrell were assistant directors. On 1 August 1978, John Lane, an under secretary in the Department of Transport was appointed by the Prime Minister, on promotion to deputy secretary, to succeed John Boreham as deputy director of the Central Statistical Office. Around the same time Alec Sorrell was appointed principal director of statistics in the Departments of the Environment and Transport in succession to Geoff Penrice.

In March 1979, Barry Wakefield changed posts with Ken Forecast who was director of statistics at the Department of Education and Science. In the following months there were more moves at director level. Owen Nankivell left the service to take up an industrial post with Dunlop. He was replaced by Jack Wells on promotion from the Department of Trade and Industry and Consumer Protection.

The Rayner proposal was to cut the deputy director's post and two chief statistician posts. In the middle of 1981 John Lane retired as deputy director and was not replaced. At the same time Jack Hibbert left the Office to spend six months' special leave working with OECD in Paris and Eurostat in Luxembourg. Tony Rushbrook was given temporary promotion until his retirement at the end of 1981.

Jack Hibbert, following his special leave moved to the Departments of Industry and Trade in January 1982, as head of statistics division 2. Paul Dworkin moved into the post in the CSO previously occupied by Jack Hibbert and Tony Rushbrook.

So by the middle of 1981 Sir John had effectively cut his top management team of one deputy and four assistant directors to three assistant directors. Rayner had also recommended the loss of two chief statistician posts in addition to an earlier loss of a chief statistician post when the two social statistics branches were merged. The new organisation chart issued in August 1981 showed a slimline CSO reduced to 10 branches.

An additional feature introduced around this time was the introduction of financial budgets for the GSS. These preceded the financial management initiative in most Departments. Sir John recognised that these financial budgets were a necessary management tool which revealed the cost of different parts of the CSO's and GSS's work. This enabled the CSO to plan ahead more rationally and to make sure that resources were used in the higher pay-off areas.

The role of the customer was at the heart of Sir John's philosophy. He claimed 'that advertising to their customers in government is something government statisticians should do. It is not enough for them to sit and wait for business. Statisticians must stand up, walk about and talk to their customers then listen to them.' He claimed there were few examples of success in this marketing role. One that Sir John often quoted concerned a stock control model developed in order to optimise the holding of spare parts on war ships. That was done on request of the Royal Navy and was used to excellent effect. The statisticians in the Ministry of Defence were also marketing it to the Army and the Royal Air Force.

Sir John often noted that the statisticians' culture is one of being painstaking and giving careful attention to precision and clarity of detail. That of course does not go well with being unreflectively extroverted, which are among the requirements for marketing statistics. A Government Statistical Service – and a Central Statistical Office – must contain good salesmen, claimed Sir John. They may have to be different people from those who carry out the statistical work. But Sir John was sure that a better service would be provided if a fair number of staff can, enthusiastically, do both kinds of work. Sir John paid careful attention to manpower planning. A significant part of his intellectual and psychological effort went into trying to provide for future needs for key staff. There were about 500 professional statisticians in the Government Statistical Service. Every year Sir John planned for the replacement of the holder of any of the most senior and strategic 20 posts who could be expected to move or retire within five years. Sir John also identified and then planned, in broad terms, the careers of the 10 or so younger statisticians who appeared most promising. He often admitted that his plans did not work out perfectly and so he had to repeat his manpower planning exercise every 12 months.

Part of the role of the director of the CSO was to attend the Conference of Directors General of the National Statistical Offices of the member countries of the European Community. These were held twice yearly. One meeting each year was always held at Eurostat in Luxembourg and the other held in turn in one of the member countries. In 1983 it was the United Kingdom's turn to host the Conference. The venue for the Conference in the spring of that year was Leeds Castle. The heads of the Statistical Offices who participated in the Conference were: Mr de Geus (chairman and head of SOEC); Sir John Boreham, UK; Mr Diels, Belgium; Mr Skak-Nielsen, Denmark; Mr Kroppendstedt, Germany; Mr Kalambokidis, Greece; Mr Linehan, Ireland; Mr Pinto, Italy; Mr Malinvaud, France; and Mr Begeer, The Netherlands. There were also representatives of some international organisations – OECD and the United Nations.

The purpose of the Conference was for the heads of National Statistical Offices to advise SOEC on its work programme, specifically the updating of the Fifth Statistical Programme, 1982–84. The programme needed to be geared to satisfying the data needs of the policy directorates in Brussels and of the European Parliament while taking into account the resource, political and

Heads of Branch 1978. From left clockwise: Tony Rushbrook, Ian Beesley, Owen Nankivell, Peter Kenny, John Boreham, Sir Claus Moser, Deo Ramprakash, John Lane, Julian Calder, Alec Sorrell, Barry Wakefield, Michael Lockyer, John Ludley, Brian Mower, Ian Arnison.

technical constraints on National Statistical Offices. Such collective consultation through the Conference was invaluable in helping to ensure that these objectives of relevance and feasibility were achieved.

Pieter de Geus said in his welcoming speech to guests at the opening dinner:

'We have the opportunity to present delegations with our little brochure, commemorating 30 years of statistical work, first in the European Coal and Steel Community (ECSC), later in the European Community. That work is worthwhile in itself but also brings to memory the early post-war years when ECSC put an end to 1,000 years of enmity between different states in Europe. This important political fact, often overlooked or forgotten, is still the best thing that could have happened.

Working together as 10 member states, plus international bodies, is a contribution to mutual understanding. Also to this end we promote co-operation with developing countries in the context of the United Nations. Inis Claude (peace researcher, one of the few deserving to be called a scholar in that field) spoke of "peace through institutionalisation" in which he included all the fora where representatives of nations of the world meet, enhancing mutual understanding and co-operation. It was his belief that this brought about a lessening of tension in the world and eventually, in the long run, world peace. I would hope that our Conference, besides dealing with statistics, is a humble contribution to this mutual understanding and appreciation of each other's views.'

Ken Mansell.

Paul Altobell.

The Conference gave special attention to energy statistics. The United Kingdom emphasised the importance of good information about energy prices. Sir John Boreham said: 'That one of the most valuable things that Eurostat, with the help of National Statistical Offices, could do would be to settle a basis for compiling reliable and timely data about international energy prices.' The United Kingdom also stressed the need for better statistics on energy conservation and savings.

The Conference was very interested in Mr Kroppendstedt's description of the circumstances that led to the cancellation of the German census earlier in 1983, under possible lessons for the future. It seemed that the main point of attack on that census was the absence of 100 per cent segregation between census material and its use in administration.

Sir John Boreham's international role was also prominent in the Conference of European Statisticians (CES). This was one of the five regional commissions of the United Nations system. At its meeting in 1983–84 it considered the role, purpose and implications of analytical and parastatistical work in statistical agencies. It also considered the legal and technical instruments for the protection of data and of privacy, and consequences on the statistical use and the linkage of data banks. At the meeting in 1983 Sir John Boreham was elected to serve as chairman of the CES Conference in both 1984 and 1985.

In 1983 we saw another move of senior staff. Paul Dworkin moved to the Department of Employment to replace Guy Carruthers who had retired. Dworkin was replaced by David Flaxen on promotion to assistant director.

Sir John always recognised that the CSO's first objective was to provide government with a statistical service as a vital ingredient of its administrative and policy consideration. A seondary role, was to provide the best possible service to users outside government. In this respect Sir John indicated that the CSO, as one of its functions, was equivalent to a medium-sized publishing house. The annual sales of CSO's publications totalled some 25,000 copies of annual publications and 125,000 copies of monthlies and quarterlies. This represented an annual turnover of £$^1/_2$ million.

Sir John indicated that:

'While it could be said that every table of statistics spoke for itself, some of them used bad language. So, to enable our customers to extract the most information from bald figures and examine the reasons for fluctuations in trends, we must also offer an intelligent unbiased interpretation so that the information can be seen in its correct perspective. The impartiality of our comment is the keystone of our effectiveness.'

He once used a famous quotation, slightly changed:

'The GSS is of necessity something of a monopoly and its first duty is to shun the temptations of monopoly. Its primary office is the gathering of the figures. At the peril of its soul it must see that the supply is not tainted. Neither what it gives, nor in what it does not give, nor in the mode of presentation must the unclouded face of truth suffer wrong. Comment is free but facts are sacred.'

Tom Griffin, Chief Statistician on international work.

David Flaxen.

91

The criteria set for the CSO's publication policy for deciding what should be published were rigid. They included quality, relevance, interest and comprehensibility. One of the most important of them was that the data should not conflict with any explicit or implicit undertaking about confidentiality made to the provider of the information. We have to show that we can be trusted. Sir John was convinced that the integrity of the CSO's publications was accepted by the CSO's customers. He claimed that 'I am determined to maintain it. The results of some of our efforts may not always be palatable to politicians, press or public, but we do not seek popularity. We seek what we think is an accurate presentation of figures and facts, and it would not serve the national interest one iota if this basic source of industrial and social intelligence was suspect in any way. It is the Prime Minister who is accountable to Parliament for the integrity of the GSS.'

Sir John was as concerned about integrity as his predecessors. In a discussion with Sir Claus Moser, Sir John indicated that the two well known 'integrity issues' in his time were the tax and price index and the change in the basis of the unemployment figures. Sir John continued: 'I felt that they were not integrity issues. They were certainly matters of statistical management but it did not seem to me they were concerned with integrity at all.'

One of John Boreham's characteristics was that he would get around the Office to meet his staff at frequent intervals. It was not uncommon to see him doing his 'walk-about', usually on a Friday morning, to meet the more junior staff. He also partook in the annual Christmas revue, where he was noted as a talented performer. He had a great enthusiasm for cricket. He often hosted the annual staff cricket match between the CSO and GSS at a suitable pitch in Sevenoaks, after both teams had been well fed and watered at his home.

John Erritt returned to the CSO from the Ministry of Defence in early 1985 to replace Ken Forecast who had taken up a short secondment to work in the Northern Ireland Office. This was prior to Forecast's retirement in August 1985.

It was on the 31 July 1985, after 35 years in the Government Statistical Service that Sir John Boreham retired. When asked what he would say to his successor, he replied: 'You are looking after £120 million worth of spending on the statistical tool which is absolutely central to democracy. Make sure it is being well spent at all times. And the other thing is something that I am rather

Jack Wells and Alan Croxford prepare for a European visit.

boringly well known for. That is that a good statistician must be at least as good with words as he is with figures. It is no good just delivering figures, we have got to deliver them in words.'

CSO v GSS cricket match. Reproduced with permission of *Sevenoaks Chronicle*.

CHAPTER VIII

THE HIBBERT
YEARS

Sir Jack Hibbert.

The Prime Minister, Margaret Thatcher, approved the appointment of Mr Jack Hibbert to succeed Sir John Boreham as director of the Central Statistical Office and head of the Government Statistical Service from 1 August 1985.

Jack Hibbert was educated at Leeds Grammar School and the London School of Economics. After National Service in the Royal Air Force he joined the Exchequer and Audit Department in 1952 and transferred to the Central Statistical Office in 1960. In the CSO he worked in several fields of economic statistics including public expenditure, capital formation and balance of payments. He was promoted to chief statistician in 1970 and was appointed assistant director (Grade 3) of the National Income and Expenditure Division in 1977. He spent a period on loan as a consultant to OECD and Eurostat in 1981. On his return in 1982 he joined the Department of Trade and Industry as head of statistics division 2.

The cutbacks in the CSO in the four years prior to 1985 were now well established and the office was going through a period of consolidation. In his inaugural address to staff Hibbert indicated how he believed the CSO's and GSS's roles might change and develop.

'I am, of course, as concerned as my predecessors with the maintenance of our professional standards and integrity. Maintaining these standards involves more, however, than ensuring that we are objective in our work. The value placed upon the statistical service we provide ultimately depends on our ability to communicate effectively with the users of that service, not only in order to establish our customers needs, but also to ensure that the statistics provided are properly interpreted. All these functions are part of the work of the GSS and we must make sure that this work is done well, if our professional reputation is to be maintained.

Maintaining these standards is not easy. Reconciling the demands for reliability and timeliness with the need to minimise costs and the burden on form fillers may sometimes seem to require the judgement of a Solomon. But our decentralised statistical system means that we can work very closely with our customers and find solutions which are based on a proper understanding of their operational needs. Good working relationships with the users of statistics are clearly an essential part of an effective GSS.

I have several ideas for strengthening the GSS and increasing its effectiveness. These ideas will need to be discussed fully, both within the GSS and within Departments, before any of them can be implemented. The changes currently taking place in the Civil Service also need to be taken into account in thinking about the possibilities for the GSS. They provide us not only with challenges but also with opportunities.

The demand for our services continues to increase. Many of our problems stem, in fact, from the difficulties of reconciling the pressures arising from this demand with our responsibilities for ensuring that the cost of meeting it represents value for money. We are able to respond effectively to that challenge because we have built up a body of skilled people who really care about their work. It is a constant source of reassurance to me when I see how deeply committed individual members of the GSS are to maintaining professional standards and integrity, and how determined they can be to see a job through to a satisfactory conclusion.'

There was a fundamental change in 1986 and 1987. The quality of the national accounts deteriorated. Wide discrepancies opened in the three measures of GDP. The 'balancing item' is the difference between the financial surplus or deficit as measured by income and expenditure accounts and as measured by the financial accounts. For some sectors this grew unacceptably large. The Treasury and Civil Service Select Committee considered the problems which poor quality statistics played in the 1988 Budget judgements. The committee recommended:

'We regard the problems of official statistics as sufficiently serious to warrant a thorough review. Accordingly we recommend the government undertakes an investigation into the operation of the various Departments involved in the collection of national accounts statistics with a view to improving their reliability.'

On 22 June 1988, the government response to the Treasury and Civil Service Select Committee report was:

'The government shares the committee's concern about the quality of national accounts statistics. While keeping in mind the related issue of minimising the burdens on those who provide statistics it has established a review to be conducted as an efficiency scrutiny led by the Cabinet Office with the following terms of reference:

CSO Christmas Party 1986.

"To examine the present interdepartmental arrangements for the production of government economic statistics and to make recommendations for achieving cost-effective improvements where necessary."

As a major compiler of economic statistics the Department of Trade and Industry will be conducting a complementary review of its business surveys.'

The scrutiny was to be carried out within the Cabinet Office. The review was led by Stephen Pickford, senior economic adviser, who was assigned to the Cabinet Office from the Treasury for the scrutiny. Other members of the team were: John Cunningham, Efficiency Unit; Robin Lynch, Central Statistical Office; Jennifer Radice, Office of the Minister for the Civil Service; and Graham White, HM Treasury.

It was intended that the report on statistics should be completed by mid-November 1988 and submitted to Sir Robin Butler, head of the Civil Service.

As the review proceeded the quality of the national accounts did not improve. The Treasury, in its publication *The Autumn Statement 1988*, summarised what it saw as the main difficulties with the national accounts. It indicated that it was difficult to assess how strongly the United Kingdom's economy had grown over the past two years because of the considerable disparity between the various measures of real GDP. The output measure, which is the most reliable short term indicator, grew by six per cent in the year to the first half of 1988. The income measure was also showing strong growth. By contrast, the expenditure measure of GDP grew by only $2^{1}/_{2}$ per cent over the same period. To the Treasury it seemed likely that aggregate expenditure had been under-recorded over the past two years.

The Autumn Statement 1988 also indicated that large balancing items had emerged in the sectoral financial accounts. Sectoral balancing items are the differences between net acquisition of financial assets as measured from financial data and income and expenditure data. In 1987 the balancing item for the personal sector was about eight per cent of personal disposable income. The financial accounts suggested that the personal sector may have acquired far more financial assets than the current and capital accounts estimates implied. This could have been explained in part by some under-recording of personal sector income.

There was a large balancing item in the first

Alan Croxford, Bob Cavanagh, Wes Townsend and Ian McKinney.

half of 1988 of about £7 billion in the overseas sector. This indicated that there were either unrecorded net inflows in the current or capital accounts, or both. To the extent that it might reflect unrecorded net current account credits the true deficit would be lower than the recorded figures.

The balancing item for the industrial and commercial companies sector also implied the likelihood of some under-recording of spending on investment and stocks or over-estimation of company incomes.

The Pickford Team conducted their scrutiny by interviewing users in government Departments, the Bank of England, firms and employers' representative bodies, City institutions, research organisations and academics. The team also interviewed producers of statistics in the Central Statistical Office, the Department of Trade and Industry, Business Statistics Office, Department of Employment, Department of the Environment, Bank of England, Inland Revenue, and Customs and Excise. They extended their interviews to people with other interests, including the Enterprise and Deregulation Unit in the Department of Trade and Industry, market research companies, the OECD and Eurostat.

The interview programme revealed an extensive awareness of problems with macro-economic statistics – discrepancies between the three measures of GDP; large and growing balancing items; and frequent and major revisions to statistics. The interview programme, however, provided little analysis of the cause of the problems or possible solutions. The review team indicated that the problems were deep seated and pervasive, had multiple causes, and had existed

Sir Jack Hibbert's Private Office 1990.

for a long time. The review team indicated a number of areas where improvements were needed or where further work was necessary. However the team did not believe that these improvements would be sufficient to solve the underlying problems. Nevertheless they made recommendations in three areas:

Changes to the way macro-economic statistics are collected or compiled.

Further work on statistical issues, in order to identify additional improvements to statistics.

Changes designed to create a statistical organisation more likely in future to meet the needs of users in a cost-effective manner.

The team made 17 recommendations concerning the collection of statistics, 14 recommendations aimed at future improvements and five recommendations concerning the organisation of statistics.

On the recommendations concerning organisation, the Pickford Team, in the report delivered to Sir Robin Butler on 18 November 1988, indicated:

'The recommendations will require consideration of machinery of government issues. We recommend that consideration of these issues should be completed by January 1989. From the point of view of improving the quality of macro-economic statistics, we recommend that:

a. BSO and parts of DTI S1 division should be integrated completely in a joint unit primarily responsible to CSO.

CABINET OFFICE

Government Economic Statistics

A SCRUTINY REPORT

by
Stephen Pickford
John Cunningham
Robin Lynch
Jennifer Radice
Graham White

LONDON: HER MAJESTY'S STATIONERY OFFICE

b. The functions currently carried out by parts of DTI S2 division dealing with visible trade statistics should be brought into the CSO, with Customs and Excise continuing with their current role.

c. The functions of DTI S2 division which relate to invisibles and other financial statistics should be transferred to the CSO; but the Bank of England should continue to collect monetary sector data.

d. The CSO should assume responsibility for the retail price index and the family expenditure survey.

e. The CSO, enlarged and reorganised as recommended above, should be established as a next steps agency; either as a separate Chancellor's Department or as an Agency of the Treasury.

f. The CSO as an Agency should have specific objectives for minimising the statistical burdens on businesses.'

The review team, in their report, could give no clear reasons why the figures had deteriorated during the 1980s. The scrutiny cited a growth in the service sector where the figures were weaker than for production, the 'Big Bang' of November 1986 and the general pace of economic growth as reasons why accuracy had diminished. The review team probed Departments to find out whether the Rayner Review which cut back

Alan Tansley in Central Government accounts. Longest serving member of CSO in 1990.

statistics in 1980 had been too drastic. The response in general was that it was difficult, if not impossible, to separate out the effects of the Rayner cuts from the general reduction in the size of the Civil Service over the same period. Some of the cuts were offset by the introduction of better computers and IT equipment. More than one Department made the point that one cause of the deterioration had been the growth in deregulation and the continued pressure to reduce the number of forms sent out to businesses, and one Department was in no doubt that the quality of their statistics deteriorated as a result of the implemention of the Rayner recommendations. The review team, however, concluded that it was unlikely that the effects of the Rayner Review had been to cause a deterioration in macro-economic statistics.

The Machinery of Government Review looking at the Pickford Recommendations on aspects related to organisational issues were considered by Jonathan Spencer of the Cabinet Office. The decision to set up an enlarged CSO was announced by the Prime Minister on 5 April 1989 in answer to a Parliamentary Question by Mr Terence Higgins. The Prime Minister said:

'Following the Treasury and Civil Service Select Committee's report on the 1988 Budget, the government set up an efficiency scrutiny in the Cabinet Office last June to examine the present interdepartmental arrangements for the production of government economic statistics, and to make recommendations for achieving cost-effective improvements where necessary. The report of this scrutiny has been published today and copies have been placed in the library of the House.

The scrutiny report recommends a large number of specific ways of improving the quality of government economic statistics, the great bulk of which have been accepted. They will be implemented over the next year under the supervision of the director of the Central Statistical Office. Copies of the Action Plan relating to these recommendations have been placed in the libraries of the House.

The report also makes a number of recommendations for changes to the present interdepartmental arrangements for producing economic statistics. In accordance with these, I have decided that from July responsibility for the Business Statistics Office and for all the statistical services for which the Department of Trade and Industry is now responsible and for the retail prices index and family expenditure survey, for which the Department of Employment is currently responsible, should transfer to the Central Statistical Office. The enlarged Central Statistical Office will have greater direct responsibility for the compilation of the national accounts and for the associated data collection from business.

As recommended by the scrutiny report, the enlarged Central Statistical Office will become a separate government Department responsible to the Chancellor of the Exchequer and in due course will also become an Executive Agency. The director of the Central Statistical Office, as head of the Government Statistical Service, will continue to have access to me on matters concerning the validity and integrity of government statistics.

The government remains committed to reducing the burdens on business involved in the collection of economic statistics. The Secretary of State for Trade and Industry, who has lead responsibility for deregulation policy, will therefore agree with the enlarged Central Statistical Office's specific objectives to ensure that burdens on business are minimised.

These decisions amount to a very substantial programme of work over the period ahead, designed to achieve a significant improvement in the quality and relevance of government economic statistics.'

The reaction to the announcement of an

Computing at CSO Newport.

John Erritt, Deputy Director.

Paul Dworkin.

enlarged CSO was largely favourable. However, the fact that the new CSO would be responsible to the Chancellor raised concern, in that there was a risk that the Treasury might manipulate data. The Treasury and Civil Service Committee examining the CSO reorganisation took evidence from the Treasury and from Jack Hibbert on 12 July 1989. The chief economic adviser to the Treasury said in evidence that while he reserved the right to criticise the CSO's product as a principal user of its output, he would not seek to tell CSO how to do its job. In earlier evidence, Mr Jack Hibbert said that if he were in the unlikely position of being pressured by a Minister to do something he thought improper he would tender his resignation.

The merger of the Business Statistics Office, parts of Department of Trade and Industry statistics divisions and part of the Department of Employment statistics division with the CSO took effect from 31 July 1989. The CSO staff increased on that day from just under 170 to around 1,000. This was probably the most dramatic development to have taken place in the history of the CSO since its birth in 1941. It brought together in a single organisation the work of collecting a wide range of economic and financial statistics with the work of compiling the national accounts. It enabled the CSO to determine priorities which were more focused to the requirements of the national accounts.

Jack Hibbert's new organisation had five directorates. John Erritt was appointed deputy director of the CSO and head of Directorate A. His responsibilities included GSS management and policy, social statistics, international relations, methodology, survey control and classifications.

The head of Directorate B was Neil Harvey who was responsible for the short term production inquiries, the annual census of production, inquiries into stocks and capital expenditure, inquiries into distribution and services, for maintaining the Register of Businesses, and for the major computing operation within the new Department in Newport. Reg Ward became head of Directorate C in charge of national accounts co-ordination, GDP estimates and public sector accounts. John Kidgell was head of Directorate D in charge of the balance of payments and financial accounts. Paul Dworkin was head of Directorate E responsible for information systems and strategy, retail prices, family expenditure survey, press, publications and publicity. In addition a small team was set up headed by Robin Scott responsible for national accounts quality control.

As the enlarged CSO was created as a new Department responsible to the Chancellor it could not rely on existing arrangements for its personnel, financial and office services. A new principal establishments and finance officer, Mr Frank Martin, was appointed on secondment from the Treasury. He had the unenviable task of arranging the accommodation, finance and transfer of personnel from three Departments and to create the working environment for the new organisation. At the same time production of the statistics had to be maintained and the Pickford recommendations followed up.

Jack Hibbert was well aware of the complexity which the merger imposed. In October 1989 he expressed his appreciation for the tremendous effort put in to making the reorganisation go so well. He was appreciative that the work in

Neil Harvey.

John Kidgell.

producing the output of the Office was not disrupted by all the changes. He indicated that:

'On the surface we presented a calm and efficient face to the world. People outside the organisation hardly seemed to notice the join between the old CSO and the new CSO, which is how it should be.

Below the surface I know the effort this entailed; it does everyone the greatest credit. I am also aware it hasn't been and isn't all plain sailing. But we are getting there.'

One of the major obstacles three months after the new Department was set up was that its financial position as a Department was still under negotiation. Frank Martin was working to put in place the systems which were needed to run the Department's finances. He was also addressing a number of personnel management issues.

Jack Hibbert introduced a new top management unit. This was quickly established. At the top was the CSO Policy and Management Committee which Hibbert chaired with the other members being the deputy and assistant directors, and the principal establishments and finance officer. It was intended that the Policy and Management Committee should meet monthly to consider the broad direction and management of the CSO.

Jack Hibbert had several meetings with the Chancellor of the Exchequer, Mr Nigel Lawson, after the merger. Jack indicated that the Chancellor of the Exchequer:

'has confirmed his keen interest in improving the statistics we issue, and this is the major task in the months ahead. We have, I think, emerged from our first weeks of reorganisation with our reputation, integrity and objectivity not only intact but enhanced. Amid all that has happened there hasn't been the slightest hint that the CSO's standards have suffered or been compromised. It must be a major concern of us all to keep it that way.'

The recommendations made, especially about reorganisation, enabled the CSO to focus its priorities more clearly on difficulties with the national accounts. It was in early 1990 that a new set of priorities for the work of the CSO was established. This was shortly after Jack Hibbert was knighted in the New Year Honours List.

When the Chancellor of the Exchequer, John Major, appeared in front of the Treasury and Civil Service Committee in April 1990 he was asked by the chairman: 'How much of the uncertainty about prospects and the efficacy of policy instruments do you think is attributable to the continuing poor quality of economic statistics?'.

The Chancellor of the Exchequer replied:

'Yes, I am concerned about the statistical base. I think there is absolutely no doubt about that, both because we need that for forecasts and because we also need the best level of statistics we can get for measurement and what precisely is happening at any particular time in the economy. We have looked at some statistical changes. I am now considering what else we can do. Though I have not yet reached conclusions to improve the general statistical base I think that is both desirable and

necessary. It is a matter I am discussing with the director of the Central Statistical Office and I have asked for his advice and a paper from him as to what we can do to improve the general quantity and quality, particularly the quality, of economic statistics. I do so for both the reasons I mentioned a moment ago; clearly it is important for forecasting reasons, also it is important for monitoring reasons. If, for example, we had been able to monitor more accurately the growth of demand in 1987 and 1988, it would in retrospect have been extremely helpful. I think for both of those reasons the best quality statistics we can get are clearly important. One of the additional points I would add about that, if I may, is that it is an immensely difficult proposition always to get precisely the right statistics and the right judgement.'

The Treasury Committee welcomed the Chancellor's intention to address this problem. In its report the Treasury and Civil Service Committee said:

'We believe that the interchange of papers between the committee and the Treasury has been fruitful but further progress needs to be made urgently. We intend to return to this matter as soon as the director of the CSO has reported to the Chancellor.'

Press Office.

Sir Jack Hibbert discussed a package to improve economic statistics with the Chancellor of the Exchequer to meet some of the deficiencies which Treasury officials wanted addressing. On 17 May, the Chancellor of the Exchequer announced a package of measures to improve the quality of economic statistics. In a written answer to a Parliamentary Question by Mr Terence Higgins, the Chancellor said:

'I have arranged for the Central Statistical Office to take further steps to improve the quality of statistics in three areas – services, companies and balance of payments. My aim is to introduce these changes as quickly as possible so that some results will begin to appear in the figures as early as the end of this year. This is the development made possible by last summer's reorganisation of the CSO which was undertaken to enable improvements to be made to economic statistics. On services, I propose that extensions are made to quarterly inquiries of turnover in the service industries, and that more information on external trade in services is collected on a quarterly basis. On company statistics, I propose to obtain more quarterly information on capital expenditure, stockbuilding and profits. On balance of payments (and other financial) statistics, I propose that the quarterly direct investment inquiries should be expanded, and that more information be collected about United Kingdom companies' financial transactions with domestic and overseas residents. Because of the severe problems with balance of payments statistics, I have asked the CSO to undertake a thorough review over the next 12 months of the way in which these statistics are collected and compiled.

In addition, I have asked the CSO, in consultation with appropriate bodies, to consider the case for wider use of statutory surveys. This should improve the quality of statistics by increasing response rates. It should also ensure that burdens on business are shared more fairly.'

The package of improvements undertaken as a result of this initiative included more than a dozen components. There were three important elements in the package. First, statistics on the output of the service industries were poorly based. Some information was obtained from the

Press Notices.

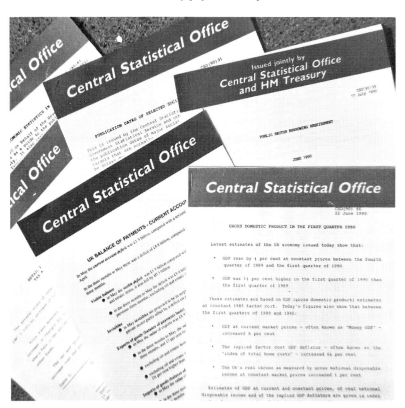

VAT system, some from employment proxies and some from inquiries. Recognising the poor coverage of this growing sector of the economy, large scale quarterly inquiries covering the service sector were introduced. The expenditure measure of GDP was of concern as it showed slower growth than the output measure; to partly rectify this and to improve the coherence of the industrial sector, the investment and stockbuilding inquiries were enlarged and made statutory. Also to improve the company sector accounts, better profits figures were sought. The final element in the package was to improve the balance of payments accounts which had shown large balancing items in recent years. The proposals here were for a concentrated effort reviewing the entire account as well extending inquiries into trade in services. The package was a substantial one calling for a hefty investment in resources. About 90 more staff were planned to be introduced, phased in during the CSO's 50th year. Improved results were expected to be delivered through 1991.

At the same time as the debate about the quality of economic statistics there were several attacks on the integrity of statistics. There was much scepticism about official statistics and how they were being interpreted. Sir Jack Hibbert indicated that government statisticians should not be too surprised or aggrieved about this; it could be seen as a sign of a healthy society. He continued, however, by saying:

'It is my aim as head of the Government Statistical Service to ensure that statistics are accepted as an objective representation of the facts.'

Sir Jack was concerned about the openness of the way the GSS conducted its work indicating that:

'We are always completely open about the methods used to compile the figures. Openness can take the form of a publication such as National Accounts: Sources and Methods, *and technical notes included in regular and* ad hoc *statistical publications; or in response to questions over the telephone. We have nothing to hide and will always be willing to make such information available provided time and the cost of doing so permits.'*

Public confidence in official statistics is affected by a number of different factors. Sir Jack indicated:

'There may simply be doubts about the quality and adequacy of the statistics being collected and disseminated. In recent times considerable attention has been focused on the apparent inadequacies of official macro-economic statistics where known errors and omissions have reached levels which made it difficult to judge with sufficient confidence what had been happening to the key macro-economic aggregates. In this instance any lack of confidence in these statistics by outside users and commentators or the general public was shared by users inside the government and action has been taken aimed at tackling the problem underlying this unsatisfactory situation.

Questions may arise, however, where the need for improvements in official statistics is not so clear cut. Government may judge that for the efficient conduct of its business certain statistics are adequate, while others outside government argue that the data available are inadequate for their purposes. Clearly the government statistician has an important role to play in situations of this kind since the judgement to be made on adequacy will have technical and value-for-money aspects to it, and in reaching a decision the government will need to take account of the professional advice given to it on these matters. Equally clearly, however, final decisions about adequacy rests with government Ministers and not with members of the GSS.'

Sir Jack Hibbert recognised that the world may change and that the definitions or interpretation of statistical series need to reflect the change. He said that:

'Such changes tend to be viewed with the greatest suspicion, even though we are at pains to publicise the fact that they are being made and to explain the reasons for making them. To give just one example, the change in the basis of the monthly indicator of unemployment in 1982, from those registered at Job Centres to those claiming benefits, was made because it was thought that the

Heads of Branch Meeting in 1990.

number registered at Job Centres could no longer provide a satisfactory indicator. In 1989 the monthly average of those registered at Job Centres was less than 150,000 compared with the claimant account of well over 2 million. Despite this, and the fact that the series on the new basis of the claimant account had been made available for periods prior to 1982, criticism of the change made in 1982 still persisted eight years later.'

It is clear that government statistics remain a topical and highly important issue as the CSO enters the 1990s. That they are important was highlighted in the first issue of the *Treasury Bulletin* in July 1990. An article entitled 'Official statistics in the late 1980s' concluded:

'Everyone benefits, directly or indirectly, from reliable and timely statistics: the government for policy making; businesses for their decision taking; and individuals, through the greater effectiveness of both government and business decisions and more informed public commentary. It must always be recognised that measuring an economy as complex and fast changing as the UK economy is not an easy task. But, difficult though it is, we must do better. It should be clear that a high priority is attached to remedying the current weaknesses in statistics.'

That they remain under public scrutiny and a matter for topical debate was also evident from the Report of a working party of the Royal Statistical Society under the chairmanship of its president, Sir Peter Moore. The report recommended further centralisation of the CSO, an idea rejected by the government in its subsequent response to Sir Peter Moore. The report considered the question of the integrity of government statistics and statisticians, but could find not a single instance of a failure of integrity. This was an encouraging endorsement of the continuing professionalism of government statisticians. Sir Jack Hibbert is firmly committed to developing interchanges of ideas and other links with statisticians outside government to make the work of the CSO more effective.

As Sir Jack Hibbert is still in office at the time of the 50th birthday of the CSO it is too early to assess the impact of the changes made during his tenure. That must be left for future historians. However, he must go down as making and implementing some of the biggest changes in the CSO's 50 years' history. The greater centralisation of economic statistics and the subsequent expansion of the CSO was unparalleled in its short history. Sir Jack's aim was to make substantial improvements in the national accounts to meet the needs of its principal users. He took a number of steps, especially in 1989 and 1990, to improve the quality of the raw data, to improve the coherence of the accounts and to provide a bespoke service to Treasury users. However we can only assess the success of his policy in part. Much of what is planned will be delivered in 1991 and beyond.

CHAPTER IX

BUSINESS
STATISTICS

Looking at the CSO's family tree it is worth examining the origins of those parts which have merged with the CSO since its birth. In July 1989, the Business Statistics Office (BSO) in Newport, Gwent, with some 670 staff, together with other parts of the Department of Trade and Industry's statistics divisions merged with the CSO. Thus the largest part of the CSO in 1991 has only a very short history within it. However, its own history is fairly lengthy.

The Business Statistics Office was set up in 1969 within the Board of Trade and it is to that Department we have to turn to discover its origins. Chapter II showed the importance of the Board of Trade in the development of economic statistics in the nineteenth century. The Board of Trade's statistical department was one of the foremost statistical departments in government, being set up in 1832 and headed by George Porter. He was succeeded in turn by Albany Fonblanque, Richard Valpy and Robert Giffen. The real background to the origins of the BSO certainly stems from those early days but, more appropriately, its start was with the creation of the Census of Production Office in 1907.

Around the turn of the century, the government collected little information about industrial activity. The need for better information about industry was recognised when

The BSO under construction in 1970.

questions on tariff policy were attracting the attention of the country and Parliament, in 1903 and 1904. It was this need that prompted the government of the day to seek the approval of Parliament for taking censuses of production to provide a more informed background against which this important economic question could be discussed.

Legislation was introduced to the House of Commons by the president of the Board of Trade, David Lloyd George, on 16 May 1906 under the ten minute rule, when speeches are usually limited to one from the introducer of and one from the opponent to the bill. On this occasion, no one rose to oppose and the explanatory statement of the president of the Board of Trade was followed by a speech by Mr Joseph Chamberlain warmly supporting the proposals. The bill was referred to the Standing Committee on Trade, which amended it in several respects. No amendments were made by the Lords and the Act received the Royal Assent on 21 December 1906.

When introducing legislation, Mr Lloyd George said: 'I propose at first that this should be a quinquennial census, but I have had representation from many quarters representing all parties, that it would be very desirable that the census should be biennial.' In the event the Census of Production Act of 1906 laid upon the Board of Trade the obligation to take a census in 1908 relating to the year 1907, and subsequently at such intervals as may be determined. In discussion in committee it was considered that the intervals at which the census should be repeated should be determined once some experience of working the Act had been

established. It was agreed that as soon as possible after taking the first census the period was to be fixed by an Order of the Board of Trade laid before Parliament, so that the final decision would rest with the House of Commons.

An amendment making the census annual was moved by Sir George Daughty and strongly supported by Mr Chiozza-Money, who argued that the whole object of the census was to trace the course of trade and that inquiries at long intervals might not be comparable owing to one occurring during a boom in trade and the other in a period of depression.

A clause in the original bill, Section 5(3), which was left by the standing committee, but

115

omitted subsequently on amendment was:

> *'The Board of Trade may, if they think fit, make arrangements with the Secretary of State and any other Department for the transfer to the Secretary of State, or that other Department, of any of their powers and duties under this Act as respects any particular industries or class of industries, and the Board of Trade and the Secretary of State, and any other Department authorised under any enactment to collect statistical returns, may delegate to a committee containing representatives of the Departments concerned, all or any of their powers and duties in relation to any such statistical return under this Act or such other enactment, as the case may be.'*

A clause such as this would have practically created a centralised statistics bureau, under an interdepartmental committee.

Section 3 of the 1906 Act, as finally passed, specified the matters about which information could be obtained. These included the nature of trade or business and particulars relating to output, the number of working days, the number of persons employed, and the amount of power used, but not wages or quantitative information about output.

The Census of Production Office of the Board of Trade was opened in 1907 under its first director, Mr David F Schloss. But illness, leading to early retirement, meant that the director spent little time in his post. The setting up of the Department was left principally to Henry William Macrosty. Macrosty entered the Civil Service in October 1884, being rather less than 20 years of age, as a 'man clerk of the lower division' (now the executive class), and was appointed to the Exchequer and Audit Department. In the early 1900s, Macrosty was a member of the Fabian Society and produced a study of the organisation of industry. This resulted in the publication *The Trust Movement in British Industry* – a detailed investigation of the state of British industry. The reputation won by his *Trust Movement* was the main cause of his transfer to the Census of Production Office. With the illness of its first director, Schloss, Macrosty was responsible for the organisation of the work, the consultations with industry and the preparation of schedules.

Macrosty was never appointed director of the Census of Production Office. That position was given to Alfred Flux. Alfred Flux was born in 1867 and educated at Portsmouth Grammar

Data prep office at BSO in 1971.

School and St John's College, Cambridge. In the early part of his university career his work was mainly mathematical but later he studied under Alfred Marshall and developed a lasting interest in economics. He was awarded the Marshall Political Economy Prize in 1889 and elected a fellow of St John's College in the same year. He took up a lectureship at Owen's College, Manchester in 1893 when he was appointed the Cobden Lecturer in Political Economy. In 1898 he became Stanley Jevons Professor of Political Economy at Owen's College, but three years later he left this country to become William Dow Professor of Political Economy at McGill University, Montreal. This post he held until 1908 when he returned to England to work at the Board of Trade on the census of production.

Flux entered the Board of Trade in 1908 as statistical adviser on the personal staff of the controller-general of the commercial, labour and statistical department. After David Schloss's retirement in the early part of 1908, Sir Henry Fountain was the acting director of statistics and it was not until 1911 that Flux was appointed director of the census.

In the work of setting up and running the census of production, Flux's right-hand man was Henry Macrosty. This was the beginning of a long, valuable and harmonious collaboration between the two men as they worked together on the subsequent censuses of production of 1912 and 1924.

The first census, for the year 1907, included all the questions specified in Section 3 of the Act with the addition for some industries of optional questions on output, machinery employed and coal consumed. The census was comprehensive, covering all manufacturing industries, public utilities, and mining industries. Smaller establishments were included as well as larger ones. The first office of the census was set up at 68 Victoria Street, London SW1. The first report was written jointly by Sir Henry Fountain and Alfred Flux and this left its mark on the subsequent censuses of production in both form and content.

In 1911 an Order was made determining that censuses should be taken in 1913 (for 1912) and thereafter in every successive fifth year. The examination of the results of the 1912 census were still in progress at the outbreak of the First

286   Ch. 49.   *Census of Production Act*, 1906.   6 Edw. 7.

CHAPTER 49.

An Act to provide for taking a Census of Production.
[21st December 1906.]

BE it enacted by the King's most Excellent Majesty, by and with the advice and consent of the Lords Spiritual and Temporal, and Commons, in this present Parliament assembled, and by the authority of the same, as follows :

Periodical census.

1. A census of production shall be taken in the year one thousand nine hundred and eight, and subsequently at such intervals as may be determined by an order made by the Board of Trade as soon as practicable after the taking of the first census and laid before Parliament.

Central authority for and expenses of census.

2.—(1) The Board of Trade shall superintend the taking of the census, and shall, subject to the provisions of this Act, prepare and issue such forms and instructions as they deem necessary for the taking of the census.
(2) The expenses incurred, with the approval of the Treasury, for the purpose of the census shall be paid out of money provided by Parliament.

Preparing and filling up of schedules.

3.—(1) Forms shall be prepared for the purpose of being filled up by the persons specified in the schedule to this Act with such of the following particulars in respect of the calendar year next preceding the date of the census, or any prescribed part of that year, as may be prescribed ; that is to say, the nature of the trade or business, and particulars relating to the output, the number of days on which work was carried on, the number of persons employed, and the power used or generated, and relating to such other matters of a like nature, except the amount of wages, as may be found to be necessary for the purpose of enabling the quantity and value of production to be ascertained :
Provided that—

    (a) If in any case it is found inconvenient to furnish such particulars as respects the calendar year, the Board of Trade may allow the particulars to be furnished as respects some other period of twelve months or prescribed part thereof ;

    (b) In order to enable the Board of Trade to compile, as far as practicable, statistics of the net value of production without duplication, the prescribed particulars as to output may include particulars as to the aggregate estimated value of the materials used and the total amount paid to contractors for work given out to them ; and

    (c) Particulars as to the quantity of output shall not be required, except in the case of articles the quantity of which is, on their importation into or exportation

World War in August 1914 and no separate report was published. After the outbreak of war, most of the staff of the Office were dispersed amongst other Departments. The director and the assistant director, William Macrosty, went to the Board of Trade headquarters with no defined duties. Macrosty spent most of the war years with responsibility for the supply of meat from overseas to the British and Allied forces. This involved very large and complicated problems of purchase, transport and distribution. Sir Thomas Robinson indicated that the complete success of the work, carried out to the entire satisfaction of all interests concerned, was largely due to Macrosty's organising ability and untiring energy.

At the end of the First World War there was a reorganisation at the Board of Trade which brought the establishment of an independent statistical department with Flux as assistant secretary in charge and Macrosty as senior principal. From that time onwards, despite periods of apparent stagnation and depression resulting from economy campaigns and apparent lack of sympathy in higher quarters, these two men – so different in training and temperament – worked steadily together to create an organisation equipped to meet the demands for fuller information on both trade and industry. Their work won increasing prestige for the statistical department of the Board of Trade.

Macrosty remained with the Board of Trade until he retired in 1930, as did Flux, who retired exactly a century after the creation of the Board of Trade's statistics department by his predecessor George Porter in 1832. Together they conducted the third census taken in 1925 (for 1924) which gave summary results from the

1912 census. This census was conducted from offices in Great George Street, London SW1. The 1930 census moved to a new location at 20 Great Smith Street, SW1, and was the last one completed before Alfred Flux retired. Alfred Flux was knighted in 1934, the year which marked the centenary of the Royal Statistical Society.

In the early 1930s there was a revival of interest in tariff problems and this led to an extension of the powers to collect information. The Import Duties Act of 1932 included provisions for collecting statistics about industries affected by duties imposed under the Act, and it allowed information about the quantity and value of materials used and goods produced to be obtained in whatever detail was considered necessary. These provisions were extended in the Finance Act of 1933 to relate to goods covered by the Silk Duties and the McKenna Duties.

Inquiries under the Import Duties Act were made for the years 1933, 1934 and 1937. In 1938 a limited inquiry took place covering six industries which were excluded from the 1937 inquiry. The census of production for 1935 was made under both the Census of Production and Imports Duties Acts. This permitted the wider ranging power of the Import Duties Act to be used. By this time the Census of Production Office had moved to 80 Pall Mall, SW1. The Second World War interrupted work on the 1937 and 1938 inquiries with the result that only preliminary reports for the iron and steel and textile groups of industries were completed and published for 1937. The results of the 1937 inquiries for other industries were published for the first time in the 1948 census report. Results of the 1938 inquiry were never compiled.

The Census of Production Act, 1939 extended the powers of the Import Duties Act to the whole census of production field but because of the war no census was taken under this Act.

After Alfred Flux's retirement in 1932, Hector Leak took over the running of statistics at the Board of Trade. Harold Wilson (now Lord Wilson of Rievaulx) recalls that the first time he met him was in 1937. At that time Harold Wilson was working with William Beveridge on unemployment and trade statistics. To develop some ideas which he had been working on, Harold Wilson went to see Hector Leak with a letter of introduction. Lord Wilson recalls:

'He was just like his legend; keen, completely on top of his job, but most wary of letting any newcomer, especially a very young statistician, put more strain on the Board of Trade statistics than they could bear. He was like his legend too in his dress; very formal, with a stiff, turned up collar of an old style. I did not get a great deal out of him, except some fairly erudite instruction on misuse of Board of Trade's figures which he felt was a fairly general practice, especially among the new economists and statisticians coming from university.

I then saw a great deal of him during the war, both when I was in the Cabinet Office and in other economic Departments. The punctilious, accurate and speedy nature of his statistics was absolutely vital to the rudimentary planning on which the Cabinet Office had embarked, and which developed so greatly during the war.

He played a full part with Harry Campion, the first head of the Central Statistical Office during the war, in modernising the statistics, in bringing them together to form a centralised caucus of essential information and also in maintaining a fairly rigorous censorship on venturesome statistical methods by some of the new Departments.'

The next major development on the collection of industrial statistics derived from the *White Paper on Employment Policy* issued by the coalition government in 1944. It specified that among the principal classes of statistics essential for the efficient operation of an employment policy, an annual census of production was required showing 'the structure of the main groups of industries in the preceding year including, *inter alia*, details of the quantity, value of output, stocks and work in progress'.

Following this White Paper, a Census of Production Committee was set up in 1945 under the chairmanship of Sir George Nelson to consider what additional information should be collected in future censuses, and to recommend what amendments might be made to the Census of Production Act. The Nelson report was published in 1945. In parallel with this, another committee under the chairmanship of Sir Richard Hopkins reported in 1946 on the taking of a census of distribution. The recommendations both of the Nelson Committee and the Hopkins Committee were reflected in the Statistics of Trade Act, 1947, which was passed with the support of all parties.

The purpose of the Statistics of Trade Act, 1947, was to obtain information necessary for the appreciation of economic trends and provision of a statistical service for industry and government Departments. In addition to providing for short-term statistics, the Act required the Board of Trade to take a census of production for 1948 and every subsequent year, and a census of distribution and other services in any year that may be prescribed by the Board. The subjects on which information could be collected was laid down in the schedule to the Act.

Whilst work to present the bill to Parliament was progressing, a partial census of production was taken for 1946. This was done under Defence Regulations 55AA. The object was to get information about certain important industries (for example chemicals, engineering and construction). A secondary objective of the 1946 partial census was to frame questions designed to elicit the additional information recommended by the Nelson Committee, the replies being considered with a view to seeing how best to obtain such information through subsequent censuses.

The first census of production in Great Britain taken under the new Statistics of Trade Act was a full, detailed census in respect of 1948. The location of the Census Office in the planning of this full census was in Great Western House in Horseferry Road, London SW1. But a move to what was meant to be a more permanent location was made in 1948, when the Census Office moved to Neville House in Page Street, SW1.

Jack Stafford became the director of statistics at the Board of Trade in 1948. He remained at its head for no less than 24 years. Jack Stafford was born and brought up in Lancashire. He went to Baine's Grammar School in Poulton-le-Fylde and afterwards to Manchester University, where he studied economics. He then became a lecturer in economics at Manchester University from 1930 to 1938. In 1938 he was awarded a Rockefeller fellowship and spent some time at Harvard and Columbia Universities. He joined the Central Statistical Office in 1941, becoming acting director in 1946 when Sir Harry Campion spent a year at the United Nations in New York. Jack was one of the principal workers in the new CSO in its formative years. He played an active part in the discussions which led up to the 1944 *White Paper on Employment Policy*. Subsequently, he played a key role in preparing the instructions to Parliamentary counsel for drafting the Statistics of Trade Act. His appointment as director of statistics at the Board of Trade in 1948, came on the retirement of Hector Leak.

The censuses of production for 1949 and 1950 were a different type of inquiry. The information obtained was of a summary character and was of a kind which provided important aggregates for the national income and expenditure accounts and enabled the changing importance of different industries to be traced in broad terms. The census for 1951 was a full one similar to that for 1948. The censuses for 1952 and 1953 were of a simple type after the 1949 and 1950 pattern. In the 1952 census, sampling methods were used for the first time which called for returns from only one in three establishments employing more than 10 persons and one in 20 firms employing 10 or fewer persons.

In 1950 the first census of distribution was taken. The trades covered in this census were restricted to wholesale and retail distribution and a limited number of service trades including restaurants and canteens, motor trades, hairdressers, funeral furnishers, portrait photographers and boot and shoe repairers. All businesses covered in this census were required to give figures of sales, purchases, stocks, employment and wages and salaries. The census was carried out by the Census of Distribution Office. This was a new office set up in Jersey Road, Osterley in Middlesex. The taking of the census, the processing of completed forms and the issuing of reports took some three years to complete. The total staff employed at the Census of Distribution Office at its peak level in the summer of 1951 was about 700.

In May 1953 the president of the Board of Trade appointed a committee under the chairmanship of Sir Reginald Verdon-Smith to advise him about the future policies on censuses of production and distribution. This committee reported in a White Paper published in October 1954. The committee concluded that the censuses of production and distribution served a useful purpose and should be retained but accompanied this broad conclusion with a number of specific recommendations designed to make censuses more effective and to reduce the burden they imposed on the business community. Among the more important recommendations were the extension of the use of sampling methods and the exemption of a wider range of small firms from the obligation to complete detailed census of production returns.

Plans for the full, detailed census of production for 1954 were settled well before the report of the Verdon-Smith Committee was published. So a fairly detailed full census was held that year. This year saw yet another move for Census of Production Office. It was relocated from Page Street to Lime Grove, Eastcote in Middlesex. At the same time the Census of Distribution Office moved to the Eastcote site. The recommendations of the Verdon-Smith Committee were implemented for the censuses in 1955 to 1957. The questions asked related only to the more important aggregates. The forms were reduced to a single page and as far as possible the questions were framed so that the figures required could be readily derived from firms' financial accounts. The new Census Office in Eastcote from 1956 was run by a chief statistician, Hugh Stanton.

Further changes were made to the 'full' detailed census for 1958, which again included the recommendations made by the Verdon-Smith Committee. One of the most important changes was the raising of the exemption limit below which firms were not required to make detailed returns. For the 1958 returns full details were sought only from firms employing on average 25 persons or more.

The census of production for 1959 was the first of a series of simple annual censuses for the years between the detailed census for 1958 and the full census for 1963. The questions were restricted to the total value of goods sold and work done, stocks and work in progress, and capital expenditure.

Minister Michael Noble visiting BSO site in 1970.

The Statistics of Trade Act provided for the appointment of advisory committees to help the Board of Trade in drawing up plans for the census of production. The committee comprised about a dozen non-official members and met under the chairmanship of the director of statistics of the Board of Trade. The committee had representation from industry, the accountancy profession, the trade unions and universities. The aim of the committee was to arrive at an agreed view as to the form each census should take. In more recent years the advisory committee had broadened its interest into a wider range of industrial statistics than those contained in the census of production. The advisory committee still meets today.

In 1960 the statistics division of the Board of Trade comprised 788 people of whom 443 worked at the Census Office. There were 101 members of staff in the branch headed by Wulf Rudoe concerned with finance, United Kingdom trade and wholesale prices, 114 staff dealing with production statistics headed by Horace Browning, 61 staff working on statistical and economic reports headed by Nita Maton and 68 staff working under Tom Paterson on investment and distribution statistics.

In the 1960s the government was looking closely into what could be done to improve industrial statistics, both to meet its own needs and those of industry. At the same time, importance was being attached to timeliness and the desirability of working to uniform concepts and definitions. The reports from the Estimates Committee on the Government Statistical Service in 1966 underlined the desirability of developing official statistics in these directions.

To integrate effectively the various streams of industrial statistics, to secure comprehensive industrial coverage while reducing the possibility of duplication or overlap, and to facilitate the adoption of common standards and definition a new office, the Business Statistics Office was set up. The formation of the Business Statistics Office was announced by the Prime Minister, Harold Wilson, on 16 December 1968. The new Office came into being on the 1 January 1969. The director of the Business Statistics Office, was Martin Fessey who was responsible to the Board of Trade for the day-to-day work of the Office. The policy of the Office was decided by an interdepartmental management committee under the chairmanship of Claus Moser. Plans were made for the Office, which was being developed out of the Board of Trade Census Office at Eastcote, to move to Newport, Monmouthshire in stages between 1969 and 1972.

The work of the Business Statistics Office included continuing the census of production. Quarterly and monthly inquiries were introduced designed to provide statistics on the value of output of products characteristic to each industry. These statistics were supplemented with inquiries about capital investment, stocks, purchases and sales.

By the time Martin Fessey arrived at Eastcote at the end of 1968 the Census Office was dispirited. Martin indicated that the 1963 census of production had been an albatross, with those who had struggled with it for five years wondering if it would ever end.

Board of Trade statisticians in 1968. From left clockwise: Ted Steer, Bernard Middleton, Julia Weatherburn, Tony Dunn, David Harris, Hugh Stanton, Nita Maton, Guy Carruthers, Arthur Jessop, Alec Sorrell, Ron Green, unknown, unknown, Paul Dworkin, Tom Paterson, Katie Firth, Bill Wessell, Martin Fessey, Jean Thompson, Michael Lockyer, David Hutton.

Martin Fessey.

BSO Management Committee, 1977. From left clockwise: Shirley Carter, Sir Claus Moser, Laurie Berman, Owen Nankivell, Roger Thatcher, Leonard Napolitan, Alec Sorrell, Martin Fessey, Ray Ash, Geoff Penrice.

Following the announcement that the location of the BSO was to be at Newport, there was a hectic six months in which detailed specifications for a new building on the site at Tredegar Park had to be made. A report on the planning and design aspects of this new building was prepared by Sir Percy Thomas and Son, the architect responsible for this work. Originally the project was planned in two stages; the first to provide 270,000 square feet of space and accommodation for 1,300 people, of whom 800 were expected to be recruited locally. The plan for this stage was to complete a block for housing the computer by mid-1971 and for the whole of the first stage to be finished within 18 months after that. The second stage of building was expected to begin later in the 1970s. Once complete, this would permit the increase of personnel up to 2,200 and provide additional computer facilities.

Until the new building at Tredegar Park was ready, accommodation for around 250 staff was made available at Chartist Tower, Newport and for around 100 staff at Royal Chambers, Newport. The move of staff into this accommodation started on 13 January 1969 and was principally managed by a senior executive officer, Arthur Lacey. At the beginning of July 1970 some 242 staff were housed in Chartist Tower of whom 59 came from Eastcote, 83 from other Board of Trade offices and the remainder from Newport or thereabouts.

There was much speculation about what conditions would be like at the new building at Tredegar Park. The head of administration, Roy Sims, indicated some of the special design features incorporated in the building scheme.

'The main office block would be square shaped with a central landscaped court and lifts and other circulation services contained in vertical cores in the corner of the block giving large clear areas for office planning. Apart from a certain number of predetermined rooms, most of the office space is planned to allow for the maximum of flexibility in the laying out of work areas. This has been achieved by including a specially developed modular ceiling and partition system throughout all main office areas which allow prefabricated demountable partitions and light fittings to be positioned at will. Windows are continuous around the office blocks and on south-facing elevations will consist of a new type of heat rejecting glass, slightly tinted, which will reduce solar heat gain substantially. The BSO will be one of the first buildings to incorporate this glass in the United Kingdom, although it has been used before in the USA and South Africa. How nice to associate Newport with other sunny climes! Let us hope that the characteristic claimed for this glass will be thoroughly put to the test.'

At the beginning of 1973 the BSO had 903 staff. Among them were 15 professional statisticians: director, Martin Fessey; two chief statisticians, Bernard Mitchell and John Simmons; eight main grade statisticians, and four assistant statisticians. Outside the inquiry branches, the computer and management services

Cartoon from first edition of BSO Magazine.

I'M AFRAID WE'RE NOT QUITE READY FOR YOU YET. CAN YOU COME BACK NEXT YEAR?

Commemorative
plaque to mark the
opening of BSO.

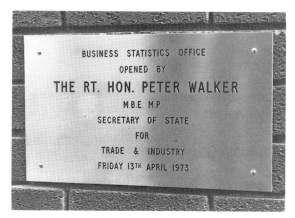

branch was headed by Jack Tiffen (assistant secretary) supported by four principals; and the administration of the Office was the responsibility of Roy Sims (senior principal).

The considerable increase in the size of the office in the early years reflected the introduction of a new centralised and integrated system of industrial statistics. In addition the third census of distribution was held in 1971 and was a major task for the BSO. The aim of the Office was that it should become the main agency for collecting and publishing industrial and commercial statistics. It was envisaged that the Office would further expand in the 1970s taking over responsibility for short-term distribution statistics and for construction statistics. An additional major task envisaged when the BSO was set up was the creation and maintenance of a central register of businesses for use by all Departments for collecting business statistics. In answer to a Parliamentary Question on the recommendations on statistical form filling in Chapter 15 of the report of the Bolton Committee on Small Firms, the then Parliamentary Under Secretary of State for Industry (Mr Nicholas Ridley) acknowledged the importance of a central register of business and stated that the Business Statistics Office was actively exploring the possibility of developing such a register. The BSO also created a new *Business Monitor* series through which as much as possible of the information collected was published. Martin Fessey's tenure as director of the Office ended in 1978. He was replaced by Ray Ash.

The climate which favoured an expansion in the collection of official statistics began to change in the mid-1970s. There were rising concerns about the cost to public expenditure and in the case of business statistics, about the cost which government imposed, particularly on small firms. The change of climate became more pronounced during the early 1980s with government policies of less intervention in industry and with cutting back the Civil Service as part of its drive to reduce public expenditure.

The number of staff at the BSO peaked at around 1,100 in 1975. It fell to around 700 between 1979 and 1986. Within that reduced total approximately 60 staff were engaged on new work transferred to the BSO during the early 1980s. The BSO successfully responded to these challenges by becoming more efficient. But the

pressures to reduce costs both to government and industry led inevitably to reductions in the volume of information collected. The changes were achieved in various ways. In the case of the quarterly inquiries concerning turnover, exemption limits affecting smaller businesses were raised. Sampling was introduced or its use extended in most of BSO annual or less frequent inquiries. Increased importance was attached to extracting as much information as possible from a smaller number of forms and register details on which the inquiries were based. Greater efforts were made to improve response rates. Considerable software developments were required to accommodate the changes in the

Visit from North Americans. Seated are Martin Fessey, BSO and Shirley Kalleck from the US Bureau of the Census.

inquiry designs and estimation procedures. In 1986 Ray Ash retired and Reg Ward became director of the BSO.

In the 1970s and 1980s there were three statistics divisions in the Department of Trade and Industry. Laurie Berman was the deputy secretary in charge from 1972 when he replaced Jack Stafford. In 1983 Hans Liesner, chief economic adviser in the Department of Trade and Industry assumed responsibility for the three statistics divisions.

The two headquarters divisions were important users of the BSO statistical output. S1 division served three main customers: the policy divisions within the Department of Trade and Industry which received extensive statistical

Ray Ash.

Romance blossomed at the BSO in 1978.

128

briefings on industrial activity; the CSO which received estimates of the index of production for industries which were the responsibility of S1; and industry and the public which needed information to allow informed judgements to be made on developments in industry.

The main work of the second of the statistics divisions within the Department of Trade and Industry was concerned with the analyses and interpretation of the United Kingdom trade statistics and the collection of information relating to company financial statistics. This division converted the detailed overseas trade statistics produced by HM Customs and Excise into a time series for incorporation into balance of payments accounts and the national accounts. Information about companies' finances was brought together from a variety of sources to build up as complete a picture as possible of the financial state of the industrial and commercial company sector.

In 1989 the Pickford Report recommended that the bulk of statistics divisions in the Department of Trade and Industry, including the entire BSO, be moved under the control of the CSO. This was to give the CSO responsibility for collecting industrial statistics which focused more on the requirement to improve the national accounts rather than the information required to monitor industrial trends. The merger with the CSO took effect on 31 July 1989. This action ended a long and voluminous history of statistics in the Department of Trade and Industry and its predecessor Department, the Board of Trade, spanning over 150 years. In its own way the move was one of the most significant events that have taken place in the history of statistics, with around 800 Department of Trade and Industry staff

Senior management at BSO in 1985. Left to right: Bernard Mitchell, Stephen Curtis, Bill Knight, Ray Ash, Cyril Maskall, Roger Norton, David Lewis.

Carnival float.

moving to the CSO where staff levels at that time were a little over 150. It marked a new era for the future of industrial statistics.

Left to right: John Astin, John Walker, Neil Harvey and Richard Butchart of DTI S1 Division.

Left to right: Bill Boyd, Graham Jenkinson, Peter Stibbard and Peter Richardson of DTI S2 Division.

CHAPTER X

PRICES AND FAMILY EXPENDITURE

The CSO statistic that affects the lives of individuals more than any other is the retail prices index (RPI). Measuring the overall change in the prices of the goods and services we buy, it is used by the government for up-rating tax rates, and by the private sector for a wide range of purposes including pay determination. It is the predominant measure of inflation. Before the 1989 amalgamation, it was produced by the Department of Employment, but the collection of retail price statistics began in the nineteenth century, in the labour department of the Board of Trade.

In 1903, Sir A E Bateman was in charge of the commerce, labour and statistical department. The department was based at 44 and 50 Parliament Street, London SW1, in buildings currently being refurbished for Parliament use. Bateman was a career civil servant, having served some twenty years in the Department. He was succeeded in 1903 by his deputy, Hubert Llewellyn Smith, who made his reputation in industrial negotiation and was in later years to be responsible (during the tenure of Winston Churchill as president of the Board of Trade) for the planning of the system of unemployment insurance, and setting up labour exchanges.

In August 1903 the statistical department produced two massive reports. One was a comparison of the costs of living in Britain with those in other countries. This showed detailed comparisons of the prices of items within working-class budgets. The report drew attention to the difficulties of ensuring a comparable specification of the products being priced.

The report contained, apart from prices, estimates of family budgets for the working class

in 1901 based on investigations carried out by private social investigators, such as Booth and Rowntree, together with the results of an inquiry undertaken by the commissioner of labour of the United States into working-class expenditure in various countries in 1891. They show a fascinating insight into the quality of life of the workers of the day.

Just a hundred years ago, the American survey took a sample of 455 British working-class families. Although this was small in comparison with today's family expenditure survey, by comparison with the privately-financed surveys being carried out in the nineteenth century it was quite large. The sample families had an average income of £1 13s 10½d (£1.69p in today's money). Of this 78p was spent on food (not including alcohol and tobacco), 23p on clothing and 19p on rent. Many of the poorer-paid relied on second-hand clothing, and some repaired their own shoes. Those with gardens would grow some of their own food, but in the 1901 census, over a quarter of London's population lived in one- or two- room tenements. The principal item of food, in terms of quantity, was bread. Some families made their own bread. A 1903 inquiry showed that the average working-class family of five consumed 32lb of bread and flour in a week, compared with just over 9lb of meat of all kinds. In addition the family bought 13½lb of potatoes.

Nevertheless, the resources of private investigators could not hope to produce a comprehensive picture. In 1904 the Board of Trade carried out its own survey of the family budgets of 1944 working-class households in urban areas. This was published in a 1904 report, which extended the coverage of their statistics to

by Vicky. Reproduced
with permission of
the *Daily Mirror*,
published 8 February,
1954.

the price of items of food, clothing, fuel and light, and rents. The report included a chart of the first index numbers of the cost of living, relating to the working classes in large towns in Great Britain for the period 1880–93. The 1904 survey is important, because it formed the basis of the weights of the first cost of living index, which ran from 1914 right up to 1947.

The second report of 1903 was a memorandum on wholesale and retail prices. For the economic historian the report is a gold mine of detailed price quotations for the nineteenth century. It was mainly devoted to wholesale prices. Prices were measured for over 80 items in a variety of locations, and indices calculated. The report also contained discussions of the methodology behind many of the indices then current or proposed. In contrast the retail prices measured were few, covering just nine items of food, and prices in London only.

Cost of Living Index (1914–47)

Despite growing interest in statistical methods it was not until 1914 that the government began making a systematic attempt to keep a continuous check on the increase in the cost of living. In July 1914 the Board of Trade instituted a regular monthly inquiry into the retail prices of the principal items of working-class family expenditure, publishing the percentage change each month in its *Gazette*. Until July 1916 the published figures related only to food prices but subsequently the index was expanded and calculated retrospectively to cover clothing, fuel and some other items.

Each issue of the *Gazette* carried the statement that:

'The result of the calculation (in which the same quantities and, as far as possible, the same qualities of each item are taken at each date) is to show the average percentage increase in the cost of maintaining unchanged the standard of living prevailing in working-class families prior to August 1914, no allowance being made for any changes in the standard of living since that date, or for any economies or readjustments in consumption and expenditure since the outbreak of the war.'

Though it was far removed from the concept underlying the modern RPI the new index was accepted at the time as a valuable aid towards protecting ordinary workers from what were initially expected to be temporary economic consequences of the First World War. A report in 1986 by the Institute of Fiscal Studies said of the cost of living index that:

'its design was one appropriate to a society that was at least perceived to be changing only slowly and whose different classes were seen as readily identifiable and homogeneous groups'.

The information used for weighting together the components of the index was crude in the extreme. Average expenditure on food and rent was obtained from a survey of urban working-class households which had been undertaken in 1904, roughly updated, but the figures for other items seem to have been little more than guesses. The weighting pattern was influenced by highly subjective assessments of what constituted legitimate expenditure for a working-class family:

beer was completely excluded and tobacco had a weight which was demonstrably far smaller than its share of average expenditure.

Nevertheless the cost of living index was far more comprehensive than anything that had gone before. It also broke new ground by introducing improved methods of price collection. Briefly these were as follows:

Food. The prevailing retail prices of some 14 foodstuffs were collected at the beginning of each month by local offices of the Board of Trade (later the Ministry of Labour) in over 600 places. For each item the percentage change in the (unweighted) average price was calculated both for the large towns (those with populations over 50,000) and for the smaller places, the index being based on the average of these two percentages. Vegetables (other than potatoes) and fruit were excluded because of the wide variations in their quality and the seasonal fluctuations in both consumption and prices.

Rent. This component of the index covered unfurnished houses of the type usually occupied by working-class families, most of which were subject to statutory rent control. Information was collected from local authorities, associations of property owners

Press collecting the RPI Press Notice.

and house agents in 38 large towns, and used to calculate the average permissible increase in controlled rents, which was then adjusted to take account of the extent to which these increases had actually been imposed. After 1928 allowance was also made for the increasing proportion of decontrolled houses and the extent to which their rents exceeded the controlled rents for similar property. From September 1939, with the outbreak of war, increases were in effect limited to the changes in rates and water charges, details of which were obtained from local authorities.

Clothing. Inquiry forms were completed by more than 200 representative outfitters, drapers and boot retailers, each of which quoted for the same articles every month (or those most nearly corresponding). The items included were those generally bought by working-class households, including dress materials and, from 1942, 'utility' goods sold at relatively low prices. Charges for making-up were obtained by a special inquiry amongst dressmakers with a working-class clientele. Because of wide variations in price and quality the index was not based on average prices, but on averages of the percentage changes shown by individual quotations. This method of coping with non-homogeneity is still used in the present index, not only for clothing but also for many other items.

Fuel and light. Information on the prices of coal, gas, lamp oil, candles and matches was collected by postal inquiry from a representative selection of retailers, the index

for each item being based on the percentage change in the average price.

Other items. This group included a wide range of goods and services. The average prices of soap and soda, domestic ironmongery, brushes and pottery were based on information obtained from retailers by postal inquiry while the percentage increases for tobacco products and newspapers were averaged , having been obtained from (respectively) the manufacturers and publishers. Railway, tram and bus fares (each for a specified distance) were supplied by the Ministry of Transport and principal operators.

In retrospect the most striking feature of the cost of living index was its heavy emphasis on 'working-class' expenditure. This extended not only to the choice of items covered but also to the specific price indicators used. For example, the cuts of beef priced were ribs and thin flank. The number and range of items included was therefore much smaller than in the present index.

However, during the period when it was being compiled, most criticism of the cost of living index centred not on its restricted range but on the fact that the relative weights attached to the constituent items remained unchanged. By then some types of expenditure were grossly overweighted (for example candles and lamp oil) while others were either underweighted or entirely excluded (for example electricity and ready-made clothing). As a result the index was widely regarded as out-of-date and inadequate.

The institution of the cost of living index in

1914 to measure changes in the cost of living of the working classes compared with pre-war days did not alleviate concern. In 1918 the Minister of Labour appointed a committee under the chairmanship of Lord Sumner to inquire into 'the actual increase since 1914 in the cost of living of the working classes, etc'. The members were Professor Sir W J Ashley, University of Birmingham; Professor A L Bowley, University of London; Mrs Knowles, reader in economic history, London; Mr Newton Smith, secretary of Edmonton Co-operative Society; Mr J J Mallon, secretary of the Anti-Sweating League; Mr Pember Reeves, Ministry of Food;

Orphanage, home of RPI from 1964 to 1988.

and Mr W Coggan, War Office.

The committee looked at budgets rather than prices or quantities alone. They concluded that working-class budgets had increased by 74 per cent during the First World War. Without the benefit of a purpose-built survey they had to put together data from various sources:

The 1904 Board of Trade survey;
Private investigators' budgets data;
A 1912 inquiry by the Board of Trade into fuel and other household goods;
Field's analysis of gas accounts;
Ministry of Food data on rations; and estimates of average consumption.

Perhaps as a consequence of the multiplicity of sources, and the problems this raised, the committee made a recommendation, which they admitted might be slightly outside their terms of reference:

'[We] ... have been greatly struck by the improvement which might be made in the value of statistics which the different government Departments regularly collect, each for itself, if some authority existed charged with the duty of keeping them all in line, ensuring the employment of uniform standards and interrelated methods and unifying the whole by the application of principles of scientific co-ordination.'

Exchange House, Watford, home of RPI team since 1988.

138

The Ministry of Labour was dismissive: 'There is nothing original in this, and there is no need to go into the arguments for and against a Central Statistical Authority,' wrote the director of statistics. In general, though, the committee's report did not cast serious doubt on the cost of living index.

Proposals for a new family budget inquiry surfaced again at the end of 1926. John Hilton was director of statistics at the Ministry of Labour. Rents had risen considerably since 1914 and he estimated that this could make a significant difference to a rebased index. The Treasury gave its sanction to an estimates provision on 27 November 1926, and plans were drawn up for a survey which would comprise 5,000 budgets collected in each of four separate weeks, covering the manual working class, lower-paid clerks and shop assistants, whose living conditions were thought to be similar. Agricultural workers were to have been excluded.

The TUC and the National Confederation of Employers Organisations (NCEO – later the CBI) were consulted. The TUC objected for two reasons. First, they believed that the economy was still suffering from post-war dislocations. Also the Rent Restriction Act was due to expire at the end of 1927, and the government had not announced whether it intended to extend the Act. The NCEO also felt that the time was not ripe, so the proposal was dropped.

The need for a revision of the index continued to be officially recognised, and in April 1936 the Minister of Labour, Mr Ernest Bevin, announced that a comprehensive inquiry would be instituted to obtain information on the current distribution of working-class expenditure. A committee was appointed to advise on methodology, chaired by Frederick Leggett, a principal assistant secretary at the Ministry of Labour. The committee included representatives of the TUC and NCEO, the Women's Co-operative Guild and the Chamber of Trade. Dr J J Mallon, by now warden of Toynbee Hall, was again appointed. From the universities were Professor Bowley (London) and Mr D Caradog Jones (Liverpool). The Minister was particularly concerned that women should be strongly represented on the committee and two were appointed, Mrs Gamley and Mrs Darling, not representing any particular organisation. E C Ramsbottom, director of statistics at the Ministry of Labour was on the committee, as were representatives of the Ministries of Agriculture and Food, Health, the Scottish Office, and the Northern Ireland Department. J G Cannell of the statistics division was the secretary.

The survey, covering more than 10,000 households, was carried out in 1937–38. It was considered so important that the Minister, Ernest Bevin, made a Ministerial broadcast on the radio to explain the purpose of the inquiry. The survey was again aimed at the working class. It covered manual workers, whatever their income, and non-manual workers earning up to £250 a year (except the self-employed). The sample was selected from insurance records, supplemented by samples from certain classes of worker (for example civil servants and railwaymen) who were exempt from unemployment insurance, and by samples selected by the trade unions and the National Federation of Women's Institutes.

However, by the time the results became available, the Second World War had begun so further action on the revision of the index was deferred, the Ministry continuing to calculate the index on the old basis. During the early part of the war the level of the index was kept relatively stable by intensive manipulation of price regulations, the cost of a few controlled commodities used as price indicators being reduced (by subsidies financed from taxation) in order to compensate for uncontrollable price rises elsewhere. Because of this, and the continuing concern about its antiquated structure, the integrity of the index was increasingly called into question during the war years and it was widely regarded as having understated the true rate of inflation.

In 1943 there was a bid to reduce the

1937 Enquiry Form. Reproduced with permission of Public Records Office.

frequency of publication of the cost of living index to four times a year. The index had been kept reasonably stable during the war, by the manipulation of controlled prices and subsidies, and it was felt that less frequent publication might ease pressure on the resources of the Ministry of Labour, and might slow down the pressure for wage increases in the working population generally. The TUC and the British Employers Confederation (formerly NCEO) were consulted. It emerged that many workers were covered by agreements under which pay rises were triggered automatically by rises in the monthly index. Reduction in frequency and the need to renegotiate all these agreements would have caused industrial havoc. The proposal was not taken further. Later that year Richard Stone, secretary of the Sub-committee on Post-War Statistics, put forward its first interim report, which implied that the construction of the cost of living index would be reviewed, but that it would continue monthly after the war.

In 1946 a new committee, the Cost of Living Advisory Committee, was set up:

'to advise the Minister of Labour on the basis of the official cost-of-living index figure and on matters connected therewith'.

The committee was chaired by R M Gould, chief industrial commissioner of the Ministry of Labour and National Insurance (MLNI). Among the members were two statisticians from the universities, ex-wartime members of the CSO Professor R G D (later Sir Roy) Allen and Richard Stone; representatives of employers, trade unions, the retail trade and Women's

Institutes; from the Ministry, R B Ainsworth, the director of Statistics; Jack Stafford, acting director of the CSO; representatives of the Board of Trade, Scottish Office and Northern Ireland; and Mrs T Cazalet-Keir and Sir Frederick Leggett, former chief industrial commissioner of the Ministry. The secretary to the committee was J G Cannell, a senior executive officer in the statistics branch of the MLNI.

The immediate question to be resolved was whether any revision of the existing index was practicable or desirable in present conditions and, if so, what revision might be made. In an interim report the committee advised that a revision was certainly desirable, as changes in consumption patterns since 1914 had made the weighting pattern seriously out-of-date, but practicability was thought to be a less straightforward question. A choice had to be made between three potential sources of weighting information: a new household inquiry; the estimates of consumers' expenditure provided by the newly-emerging national accounts statistics; and the still-unused results of the 1937–38 inquiry. The first two alternatives were rejected because the committee felt that, in the immediate post-war period, spending patterns were too abnormal and volatile to form a suitable basis for a permanent new index series and, in the case of the national accounts, because the material related to the whole economy and would not be typical of ordinary working-class households.

The committee therefore fell back on the 1937–38 results, though it was emphasised that this should only be regarded as a temporary expedient, pending the restoration of more settled conditions. The recommendation was accepted and a technical committee was set up to advise on methodology. This technical committee, chaired by Ainsworth, included Roy Allen, Richard Stone and senior representatives of the Central Statistical Office, the Board of Trade and the Ministry of Food. It recommended some fundamental changes in, for example, the selection of items for which prices should be collected and in the system of weighting to be adopted. These recommendations were carried into effect in what came to be known as the

Members of RPI team in 1990.

interim index of retail prices, started in June 1947. Many of the procedures which were established at that time continued in operation for some thirty years, and some are still in use in modified form. Thus, though by virtue of its out-of-date weighting the interim index was always regarded as no more than a stopgap, in many respects it laid the foundations of the modern index.

The expenditure pattern revealed by this inquiry was, for purposes of index weighting, adjusted to take broad account of the changes in relative prices during the war years. Allowance was also made (as now) for what was thought to have been a general under-recording of expenditure on alcohol and tobacco. Certain types of payment were not included in the weighting, primarily because of the variable or non-measurable nature of the services obtained in return. These included income tax, national insurance contributions, other insurance premiums, superannuation contributions, trade union subscriptions, expenditure on betting and cash gifts. The price changes for some other expenditure categories, most notably holidays and meals away from home, were thought to be adequately represented by the 'all items' index and were therefore not separately distinguished.

One difference between the interim index and the old cost of living index lay in the greater number and variety of items for which prices were collected. In the food group, for example, instead of the 14 articles in the old list, the interim index had about 80 items, some in several different varieties. Alcoholic drink was brought into the index for the first time, as were many services. However, given the austerity of the immediate post-war years this expansion represented no more than a long-delayed catching-up with changes in the pattern of consumption which were already well established. In comparison with today's RPI the interim index included very few luxury or leisure items.

The improvements in the structure of the index were accompanied by the establishment of better mechanisms for price collection. For the postal inquiry into clothing prices, for example, the panel of retailers was quadrupled to nearly a thousand, greater emphasis was placed on the need to allow for quality changes and, when difficulties arose over the comparability of successive price quotations, a visit was paid to the shop concerned so that account could be taken of the gradual improvement in quality which took place as economic conditions eased after the war.

Besides laying the foundations for the modern RPI the compilers of the interim index made a number of pragmatic responses to the immediate post-war situation. For example, a feature of the war years had been that beer supplies, though never rationed, were massively adulterated by dilution with water and substitution of oats and potatoes in lieu of barley. In 1947 the alcohol content per pint was far below its usual level and, as the strength was progressively restored in the succeeding years, it was felt that the increase in quality should be discounted in calculating the price change. However, the technical committee concluded that as strength was not the only criterion of quality in beer, a pro rata allowance for changes in alcohol content would overemphasise its importance to consumers, and that the price quotations should instead be adjusted to discount the extra duty payable on the greater strength. This had the effect of making some adjustment, though not a full allowance, for changes in alcohol content. In recent times changes in the strength of beer have been negligible from the average consumer's point of view so quality adjustments are no longer applied.

1953–54 Budget inquiry

Though the interim index was generally welcomed as an advance on the old cost of living index, there was widespread public dissatisfaction that it was still based on the pre-war pattern of consumption. Responding to this the Minister of Labour announced in December 1950 that he was reconstituting the advisory committee to consider whether conditions were sufficiently stable to justify the carrying out of a new full-scale budget inquiry to provide an up-to-date weighting basis for the price index. In a second interim report the committee advised that, contrary to earlier expectations, expenditure patterns had not yet stabilised. On the other hand it felt that some permanent changes had already emerged, as a result of such factors as the redistribution of income since 1937–38, the extension of Social Security benefits and changes in habits and tastes. Even though further changes were in prospect it seemed unlikely that these would be in the direction of restoring the pre-war situation. In these circumstances the committee thought that weights based upon a new budget inquiry would be more satisfactory and acceptable to the public than the existing weights, and it was recommended that a full-scale expenditure survey be undertaken as soon as possible. The committee went on to suggest that, following on from the main survey, smaller-scale budget inquiries should be mounted at frequent intervals.

The forthcoming budget inquiry was to cover a sample of the household population, though some of the information might not be used for index weighting purposes. It was felt that comprehensive expenditure data would be valuable, and there was some suggestion that it might also be used to measure the effect of price change on groups not covered by the official index. However, the committee insisted (on that as on several subsequent occasions) that there should be only one official index, as producing more than one might create confusion in the public mind. This was in response to suggestions that indices be compiled for socio-economic groups other than the working class (eg 'middle-class households' and 'salaried workers') or for particular geographical areas. The committee nevertheless recognised that information about the expenditure patterns of particular groups was of legitimate interest, and suggested that as far as possible these should be made available from the expenditure survey.

The inquiry took place in 1953–54, by which time Ron Fowler was director of statistics at the Ministry of Labour. C T Saunders now represented the CSO on the advisory committee, but Jack Stafford was still a member, as director of statistics at the Board of Trade. The survey was the largest ever, achieving a response of 12,911 household budgets. Since then the continuous family expenditure survey has been instituted, covering around 3,500 households a year at first, but later doubled.

The new index of retail prices

Although the complete results were not published until 1957, by the beginning of 1955 sufficient information had become available from the budget inquiry to enable the advisory committee to start considering how it should be used in the construction of a new index. Proposals were submitted to the Minister a year later. These were all accepted and carried into effect almost immediately, the index of retail prices (no longer 'Interim'), having January 1956 as its reference date.

The first question the committee had to consider was which budgets should be used for weighting the new index. It concluded that the expenditure of households with high incomes should not be taken into account, partly because their response to the expenditure survey had been relatively poor, but mainly because their spending patterns were found to be different from, and more variable than, those of the generality of households. On average they spent proportionately less on food, tobacco, fuel and light, and proportionately more on services such as domestic help, education, entertainment and holidays. It was decided that the upper exclusion limit should be expressed in terms of the income of the head (rather than the total income) of the household, and that it should be set at £20 a week.

It was also decided that households with particularly low incomes should be excluded from the weighting but in this case the committee felt that neither the income of the head nor the aggregate income of the household would provide an appropriate criterion. Instead it suggested excluding retired households in which at least three-quarters of the total income was derived from National Insurance pensions, non-contributory old-age pensions or other Social Security benefits received by people over 60. (The latter included widow's and disability pensions and what was then called national assistance – since termed supplementary benefit and now income support.) These 'pensioner households' were thought to form a homogeneous group with a pattern of expenditure appreciably different from that of the average household.

The advisory committee also considered the proposal that the index should cover only those goods and services which could be regarded as basic necessities. The committee firmly rejected this – a view confirmed on several subsequent occasions. The 1956 report said:

'From time to time suggestions have been made that the retail prices index should take account of price changes only for those goods or services that could be regarded as basic necessaries. For example, it might be suggested that alcoholic

PER CENT OF *WHAT?*

by Horner. Reproduced with permission of the *New Statesman*, published 26 February, 1971.

drink, tobacco, entertainments, etc, should be excluded. In the past the index has never purported to measure price changes for necessaries only and, apart from the difficulty of defining 'necessaries' there would be many serious objections to a limitation of the index in this way. We are firmly of the opinion that, as in the past, the general design of the index should be such as to enable price changes to be measured for the whole field of goods and services over which households distribute their expenditure.

This was the first step in moving away from the concept of a 'cost of living' index, to the modern view of an index of retail prices.

Housing
The mid-1950s also saw important developments in the treatment of housing costs in the price index.

The family expenditure survey
The advisory committee's proposal in 1951 that small scale budget inquiries should be undertaken at frequent intervals was eventually implemented not by a series of separate inquiries but by a continuous one – the family expenditure survey (FES) – which was started in January 1957. Apart from its size the FES was similar to the large scale inquiry of 1953. Its first report, covering the years 1957, 1958 and 1959, was published in October 1961 and the results for 1960 appeared soon afterwards.

The collection and summarisation of the FES results was not without problems. It was the first major government statistical survey to be processed by computer, and many hard lessons were learned. The computer chosen was the DEUCE computer at the Royal Aircraft Establishment at Farnborough, which had some spare capacity at the time. The National Physical Laboratory were called in as computer experts, and they certified that the DEUCE was suitable for the job. Their estimates of computer programming and operating costs suggested that the job would be done much quicker and cheaper than the traditional punched card methods. In the event, these costs proved to have been seriously underestimated, not least because the statistical requirements became more elaborate as statisticians realised the computer's potential for sophisticated analysis. Another factor was that programmers were being recruited untrained, and learning their craft on the job. Less easy to understand, after all these years, is that the FES results were originally punched on to Powers Samas cards, as used in the Ministry of Labour's punched card installation. These were not compatible with the DEUCE, and the data had to be completely repunched.

Little wonder that the 1957 results were not available before those for 1959, and not long before those for 1960.

The chained index
In July 1961 the Minister of Labour announced that he had decided to ask the Cost of Living Advisory Committee 'to consider how the results of the family expenditure survey could be used to ensure that the weighting pattern of the index of retail prices is kept up to date'.

The FES results were used to calculate weights for the RPI based on expenditure in the four years 1957–60, revaluing the expenditure at the prices of January 1962.

The original intention had been that the smaller regular inquiries would be used to indicate when a larger 1953-style survey was necessary. In the event it was decided to update the weights annually in January, using the FES result for the three years ending in the previous June. This had several advantages; it was cheaper than carrying out a large scale inquiry, and the results would be available more quickly. Combining three years' data meant that the sample was large enough to keep sampling errors acceptably low, and that the effect of genuine but transitory fluctuations in expenditure patterns was minimised. Regular updating meant the weights did not change much at each reweighting, so that long and short term comparisons were valid. It was also felt that regular as opposed to occasional revision would more readily satisfy the public that no ulterior motive was involved, and, more generally, that it was desirable to use weights as up to date as possible.

Since 1962 the general principles of the methodology have changed little. The abolition of resale price maintenance meant that prices had to be collected from the retailers rather than from manufacturers. On the other hand, the growth of large supermarket chains charging the same price in all of their outlets meant that this information could be collected centrally.

Housing expenditure

The weight for housing in the interim index had been based on furnished and unfurnished rents and owner-occupiers' mortgage payments, the price indicators being unfurnished rents, rates and water charges. This somewhat unbalanced procedure was substantially recast for the new

Bruce Buckingham, Paul Dworkin and Don Sellwood in 1986.

index. In the first place the regular rent inquiries were extended, the sample being drawn from those households which had co-operated in the 1953–54 expenditure survey. Each household renting private unfurnished accommodation was visited about every six months while information on council house rents was obtained at similar intervals from the local authorities concerned. In view of the practical difficulties of measuring changes in furnished rents, and the relatively small proportion of households concerned, the committee recommended that rent inquiries should continue to be confined to unfurnished property.

For owner-occupiers it was decided that the weight should relate to a 'net rental equivalent' designed to reflect the rent which would be payable if the property were let. This was to be estimated from the capital value as assessed for purposes of the 'Schedule A' taxation which was then levied on owner-occupied property but, as these assessments dated from before the war, they were adjusted to take account of the change in the average level of rents since that time. The price indicator associated with rental equivalent was initially the index for the housing group as a whole, though in later years the more specific index for rent was used. Besides these 'shelter costs' the 1956 index also included, in the weight for housing and as price indicators, the cost of labour and materials for house maintenance and repairs.

Millbank Tower, home of RPI/FES and other parts of the CSO in 1990.

Special purpose index numbers

From time to time there have been suggestions for index numbers of prices relating to special groups of the population, or for regions. Successive advisory committees had been wary of creating confusion by the existence of competing measures. For example, the 1951 interim report said:

> 'We are of the opinion that there would be serious objections to the publication monthly of two or more official indices covering different social, economic, or regional groups of the community. We think that there would be real confusion if two or more official monthly indices were published. We are unanimous, therefore, in recommending that only one official index of retail prices should be published monthly.'

However in 1968, the committee thought again. They recognised that pensioners were a large and, in terms of expenditure patterns, reasonably homogeneous group of consumers whose welfare was relevant to the formulation and implementation of social policy. Two indices were introduced, for one- and two-pensioner households respectively, to be calculated monthly but published as three-monthly averages. Other pensioner households and high-income households which were not covered were concluded to be too variable and insufficiently well covered in the FES to produce valid price indices.

Regional indices
Although, as we have seen, regional comparisons were included in the original Board of Trade memoranda at the start of the century, there have never been official retail price indices for the regions. When the advisory committee discussed the issue in 1968 the technical sub-committee showed that technically they would be possible, but the parent committee could not agree on the desirability of publishing regional indices. For example, the Confederation of British Industry, speaking for employers, opposed them on the grounds that they would complicate national wage negotiations, and could have an inflationary effect. The government shared these misgivings, and, as the committee had not been unanimous, the development of regional indices was not pursued.

View from Millbank Tower.

Developments in the 1970s

During the early 1970s there was little change in the method of compiling the index, apart from the routine revision of weights and such changes in price indicators and methods of data collection as were necessary to keep abreast of the continuing changes in the pattern of retailing. By the autumn of 1973 it was felt that the RPI in its current form had been in existence for long enough for a major review to be worthwhile, and the Advisory Committee was reconvened. None of the matters considered was wholly new, but they were investigated in greater depth than ever before, reflecting the fact that the committee, having already settled the essential structure of the index, was coming to be mainly concerned with specific aspects of methodology (many of them of a technical character) rather than general principles and concepts.

One of the main items on the agenda was the RPI treatment of owner-occupiers' housing costs, as it was widely felt that rateable values had ceased to provide an acceptable valuation of the shelter afforded by owner-occupied property and that the change in value was not adequately measured by the change in the average rent paid by tenants, owner-occupied and rented houses having become quite distinct markets subject to different influences. Similar conclusions had been reached in other countries, including the United States, Canada and New Zealand. The conceptual attraction of the imputed rent approach was not questioned but the Advisory Committee concluded that, in view of the practical difficulty of applying it, the time had come to change to a method based on tangible expenditure which could be directly observed.

The method chosen was to represent owner-occupiers' housing costs by the average mortgage interest payment of index households (after deduction of tax relief). However, it was recognised that simply dividing the aggregate of actual mortgage interest payments by the number of households would not give an acceptable price indicator, and that what was required was a 'standardised' indicator which reflected just two factors – changes in house prices and changes in mortgage interest rates. With the assistance of a technical working party the committee specified such an indicator, and this was introduced at the beginning of 1975. The practical effect of its introduction was twofold. In the first place the weight attached to owner-occupiers' shelter costs within the 'all items' RPI was almost halved, since on average mortgage interest payments were much less than the old imputed rents. Secondly an additional element of volatility was imparted to the index through the use of mortgage interest rates in the price indicator.

Other innovations introduced in 1975 at the behest of the committee included two concerned with weighting. In the first place, because the sample of households covered by the Family Expenditure Survey had been doubled between 1968 and 1970, much reducing the sampling errors, it had become possible for the annual revision of RPI weights to be based on just the latest year's figures (rather than the latest three years) except in a few specific cases. Secondly a more sophisticated method was adopted for calculating the price indices for vegetables and for fruit, using internal weights for the component items which varied from month to month (within a fixed overall total) in response to the changing patterns of purchases. This prevented the index from being unduly affected by extreme price movements for individual items of greengrocery which were not in fact being consumed in significant quantities at that time of year.

Some technical improvements in the method of calculating the RPI were introduced in 1978 following a further meeting of the Advisory Committee in November 1977. The Department of Employment had undertaken some studies to determine how best to group individual price quotations for weighting purposes so as to make the best possible estimates of the overall price change. It was concluded that the form of retailing organisation was the most important factor associated with price differences but that there were also significant regional variations in some cases. Other factors, such as size of town and type of shop (eg self-service or counter service), were found to be relatively insignificant. Accordingly it was decided that where large samples of quotations were collected (eg for food) these should be grouped or 'stratified' by *both* region and form of organisation. This had been done since 1978, with one-dimensional stratification (by region *or* organisation type as appropriate) where the samples were smaller.

Some other developments during the mid-1970s were related to the RPI but did not concern the index directly. One of these was the beginning of the United Kingdom's participation in international price comparisons under the auspices of the Statistical Office of European Communities. After a 'trial run' in 1973, shortly after accession to the Community, the Department of Employment took responsibility for the United Kingdom's contribution to the comparisons made in 1975 (and at five-yearly intervals thereafter). The price indicators used for international surveys were necessarily different from those appropriate to the RPI and the work of collecting price quotations was organised separately from the regular monthly round. The link with the RPI arose partly through the sharing of knowledge and experience between the two exercises and partly through the use of detailed component indices from the RPI to update the results of international comparisons.

Developments in the 1980s

The early 1980s saw some pioneering work on the relative cost-effectiveness of different parts of the RPI price collection, which made possible various improvements in 'value for money' but also emphasised the shortcomings of the existing data processing arrangements. All the changes made to the method of constructing the RPI had resulted in a complex and unwieldy processing regime. This was computerised as far as bulk data were concerned but the computer system was highly inflexible and becoming increasingly outmoded. The use of programable calculators and free-standing microcomputers had led to some efficiency gains but it became apparent that a more fundamental solution was called for and in 1982 the Department of Employment embarked on a major exercise to design a completely new processing system covering the whole of the RPI in an integrated way. The project applied innovative technology to a data set which (at that time) was unprecedentedly large for such an application, and some teething problems were experienced in producing results to a satisfactory schedule. However, after extended trials in a small number of pilot offices, followed by a large-scale 'parallel run' in the autumn of 1985, the new system was successfully introduced in January 1986. It proved its flexibility a year later in coping satisfactorily with a major restructuring of the RPI and other changes stemming from a further series of Advisory Committee meetings.

In 1982–83 the government changed the administrative arrangements for assisting low-income families to meet their housing costs, by the introduction of the housing benefit scheme. One effect of this was that recipients of supplementary benefit had the housing component within their overall benefit separately identified, whereas previously this had not been possible. The significance of this for the RPI was that it offered an opportunity to promote consistency of treatment and conformity with past Advisory Committee recommendations by subtracting this form of assistance from total housing costs, as already happened with the rent and rate rebates granted to households not receiving supplementary benefit. Implicitly the housing assistance of supplementary benefit households had previously been regarded as an income subvention: now it became possible to treat it as a price reduction and the question was whether or not this should be done.

The method of compiling the RPI was not changed immediately, as it was felt that a purely administrative change such as this should not in itself be allowed to affect the index. It altered the channel through which housing subsidies were paid but not their essential character. However, the issue remained a contentious one and, as it could not be conclusively resolved on statistical grounds, it was decided to reconvene the Advisory Committee to consider the matter.

The committee felt that the question could not be resolved without examining afresh the whole question of how subsidies and discounts were treated in the RPI. The end result of this examination was that, instead of bringing the treatment of supplementary benefit households into line with the 'net' approach generally applied elsewhere, this approach was itself abandoned in favour of treating all discriminatory government subsidies as income subventions rather than price reductions. This change of stance did not affect subsidies and discounts which were available to all consumers or were funded by the supplier of the goods or services: these continued to be treated as price reductions. However, the change did mean that the RPI became insulated from changes in the provision of selective government subsidies which increased or decreased the costs falling directly on consumers. It could be characterised as a change of definition from 'price paid' to 'price charged', one justification being that the latter produced a clearer and purer concept of price change, measured without reference to any steps taken to give *some* consumers relief from paying the full price.

Another major issue before the committee in 1984–86 was the principle and practicalities of using mortgage interest payments as a measure of owner-occupiers' housing costs. The committee ultimately endorsed the principle but was concerned about some technical problems principally affecting the weight. One difficulty was that actual expenditure on mortgage interest was arguably being inflated by the use of mortgage funds for purposes other than house purchase. The committee therefore sought and found a method of calculating a *standardised* expenditure on which to base the weight, ensuring that it would increase if and only if there was an increase in the stock of property owned and occupied by index households and therefore in the amount of 'shelter' consumed. This technical change was important in making the mortgage interest index more robust and soundly-based but had little impact on the numbers produced, apart from a modest reduction in the weight *vis-à-vis* other items.

Another major area examined in 1984–86 was index coverage, in two aspects: firstly the goods and services regarded as being within scope and secondly the types of household on whose expenditure pattern the relative weighting of these goods and services was based. The committee recommended that a number of small gaps in coverage should be filled and confirmed the approach which had been taken in the past, basing the RPI weights on the expenditure of all except the four per cent of households with the highest incomes and pensioners mainly dependent on state benefits. One detailed change which was made in 1987, again with minimal numerical effect, was to define the high-income households excluded from the weighting by reference to the income of the household as a whole rather than, as hitherto, the individual income of the head of the household.

The most visible change made to the index in 1987 was a radical restructuring of component indices, for the first time since the inception of the RPI. These considerably altered the appearance of the range of indices published but were arranged in such a way as to permit comparisons to be made between the old and new classifications by grouping new- and/or old-style indices together. The overall number of indices published was not much altered but the effect was to make available what in current circumstances is a more useful and meaningful breakdown of the 'all items' index than that formerly provided.

Since 1987 the introduction of the community charge has made it necessary to consider whether or not this cost should be included in the RPI, as domestic rates have always been in the past. Following further recommendations from the Advisory Committee it was eventually decided that the charge *should* be included and this was done from April 1989 for Scotland and from April 1990 for England and Wales. Other matters considered by the committee during this period have included the appropriate treatment of holiday expenditure (now the only item of consumers' expenditure on goods and services which is not covered) and of certain financial services. At the time of writing the recommendations on these matters are still being pursued and have not led to any material changes in the construction of the index.

The changes which have been described in the nature and coverage of the RPI have gone hand in hand with changes in the organisation and location of the work. Until 1964 it was directed from Barnard House in Ladbroke Grove, London W11. In December of that year the work moved to Watford to be located alongside other statistics collected by the Department of Employment. So it was that the RPI moved to the 'Orphanage' in Watford. The Orphanage had been founded in 1871 and later became known as Reed's School.

During the war the Ministry of Works took over Reed's School and it became a hospital for prisoners of war. In 1939 in accordance with government instructions most of the Ministry of Labour moved out of London to Southport. It was after the war when staff returned from Southport that they were located in Watford. The new offices at the Orphanage were opened in 1946 by the Minister of Labour, the Rt Hon George Isaacs. In his address the Minister said that he noticed that the statistics department had been transferred to Watford. An old friend of his, the late Jack Jones, when MP for Silvertown, had said, 'Figures cannot lie, but liars can figure!'. He hastened to add that this did not apply to the Ministry statisticians! The Orphanage remained a home for the RPI team until the late 1980s when they moved to Exchange House in Watford. Since the merger in 1989, the statisticians responsible for the RPI and FES were relocated from Caxton House to Millbank Tower alongside other CSO staff.

CHAPTER XI

THE
FUTURE

It is tempting to speculate on how future statisticians and users will see the state of statistics at the CSO's centenary. That would be pure speculation. All that can be done here is to assess the likely direction of statistics in the next 10 years from the enlarged base it acquired in 1989 and from initiatives taken to make improvements in 1990.

It is in the nature of statistical work that from time to time problems will arise, despite the efforts of the statistician ever conscious of the need to provide statistics of a high quality. Pressure for reducing revisions to early estimates, produced in response to the demand for more timely estimates, can be expected, and indeed the bulk of the improvements made in 1990 were designed to achieve this. Also, pressure from users to deliver ever quicker high-quality accounts can be expected as users' time preferences shorten. In the next decade continued pressure to reduce public expenditure can also be expected and will lead to pressure to improve statistical techniques.

There will be changes in the future. These will stem from a number of considerations. First the focus is changing from the past approach of basing estimates on small quarterly samples and benchmarking onto annual inquiries. This suffers from the disadvantage that large revisions are often found to be necessary some two or three years after the reference period. The changes being introduced will be to make estimates on larger quarterly samples, ensuring that latest information is the best available for the monitoring of the economy.

Secondly, the approach to dealing with discrepant estimates (for example, the three estimates of gross domestic product) is likely to be developed further. Even when all the estimates have been scrutinised carefully to see whether in the light of past experience any of them should be adjusted in such a way as to reduce the discrepancies, residual differences are likely to remain. Work on the use of statistical techniques to eliminate the residual discrepancies will be extended in the 1990s. In addition, there will be pressure on all compilers of the various components of the national accounts to regard their inputs as an integral part of the large and complex account of the nation rather than as components which are simply required in their own right.

Changes may also arise from new demands for statistics. These could come from three sources. They could be generated from within government, from the European Community or from the public at large. What will these new demands be? All that can be considered in any depth are those that are emerging now and will need addressing in the early 1990s. Internal pressures could arise not only from wishing to improve quality but also to provide accounts in finer and more timely detail.

As the economic forecasters' skills at modelling improve and are further developed, a new type of statistical output may be required. It may be in the form of the conventional national accounts or outside its well-established framework. Statistics can never be regarded as an end product; they are a decision-making tool. Therefore they must be responsive to the demands of the users and be flexible to changing economic conditions prevalent in the economy.

Change will also come from our membership

Cartoon by Cummings, published 18 February, 1949. Reproduced with permission of the *Daily Express*.

"No one minds a trifling error of a few hundred million or so, but when it gets into the billion ranges, we really <u>must</u> draw the line!"

of the European Community. Already a substantial statistical programme is being developed to improve the timeliness and coverage of statistics to meet the requirements of policy makers in Brussels. Of the many developments, two fairly large changes will impact on the work of the CSO in the next decade.

A major concern for the 1990s is how statistics for trade with European Community countries will be measured. The abolition of trade barriers at the end of 1992 will encourage the free flow of goods across national borders. However, the demand for trade statistics will continue as countries will still be concerned with their national economies. This presents another exciting challenge to the statisticians in continuing to produce high quality trade figures as administrative systems are changed. Work on this is well in hand but will need constant surveillance over the next decade.

The European Community now uses estimates of gross national product as a basis for determining budget contributions by member states. The gross national product statistics are therefore receiving more attention both by the United Kingdom, to ensure that our contribution is not overstated, and by the European Community, to ensure that common standards apply throughout Europe. This will lead to the greater harmonisation and closer auditing of statistical procedures and estimates. Developments in Europe, therefore, are likely to result in considerable changes for the CSO in its quest for improvements in the 1990s.

The purpose of many of the above changes would be to produce more and more appropriate statistics. In other cases it would be to produce the same figures more quickly, more accurately or more cheaply, or a combination of these aims. A factor in achieving this will be the continued development of information technology in the 1990s. Data transmission direct to statistical offices may be a catalyst to improved quality and timeliness. Information sent directly in machine readable form will avoid the need to transcribe data thus reducing errors.

However, the future of statistics may lie in another direction. It was announced by the Prime Minister, Margaret Thatcher, in April 1989 that the CSO should become an Executive Agency. This was designed to make the CSO more responsive to customers' requirements, more accountable for its statistical service and more open about its thinking and its future direction.

The main focus of attention of Executive Agency status are first, that the work of the CSO needs to be organised in a way which focuses on the job to be done – the systems and structures must enhance the effective delivery of its statistical service. Second, that the management of the CSO needs to ensure that the CSO staff have the relevant experience and skills to do the tasks that are essential. Third, that there must be a real and sustained pressure within the CSO for continuous improvement in the value for money obtained in the delivery of a statistical service.

A requirement of Executive Agency status is that the statistical work of the CSO should be carried out within a policy and resource framework agreed with Ministers. This framework would set out the policy, the budget, specific targets and the results to be achieved. It would also specify how politically sensitive issues are to be dealt with and the extent of the delegated authority of management. The management of the CSO Agency would be held to account for the results achieved.

The framework would need to be set out and updated as part of the formal annual review with the Chancellor of the Exchequer, based on a long term plan and an annual report. Once the policy objectives and budgets within the framework have been set, management of the CSO Agency would then have as much independence as possible in deciding how those objectives should be met. The crucial element in the relationship would be a formal understanding with Ministers about the handling of sensitive issues and the lines of accountability in a crisis. The presumption is that provided management is operating within the strategic directions set by Ministers, it must be left as free as possible to manage within that framework.

We have a situation, therefore, on the 50th birthday of the CSO where customers are concerned about the quality and scope of macro-economic statistics. We have a new organisation which was put in place in 1989 and a new set of priorities determined in 1990. New demands for statistics will certainly come from the European Community and could arise from within government. To this must be added the new proposals for running the CSO once it is established as an Executive Agency. So the challenges for the CSO in the 1990s are quite enormous. They will certainly go down in a future history of the CSO as a period of change and one where staff have the satisfaction of focusing on giving a better service to others. The future for the CSO is thus a challenging one. But with deeply committed members in the CSO

there should be no doubt that the challenge will be met and at the same time professional standards and integrity maintained.

Change to Agency status.

CABINET OFFICE
JULY 1989

THE LAUNCHING OF

The "Central Statistical Office"

HEADING FOR
AGENCY STATUS

After A. M. Cassandre

Bon Voyage, CSO!

REGULAR PUBLICATIONS OF THE CENTRAL STATISTICAL OFFICE

(As at March, 1943)

A. STATISTICAL DIGESTS

	Period of issue	Contents	Circulation
1) Series A	Monthly	Statistics and charts relating to the economic situation: – Manpower – Essential Commodities – Stocks of food and raw materials – Shipping – Imports – Prices and wages	– Lord President's Committee – Ministers
2) Series B	Monthly	Statistics bearing on the developing of our war effort – Production – Machine tools – Consumption and stocks – Labour – Prices – Consumption – Finance – Transport and shipping – Foreign Trade	– Ministers – Departmental officials
3) Supplement to Series B	Quarterly	– Insured persons unemployed	– Ministers – Departmental officials

	Period of issue	Contents	Circulation
4) 2nd Supplement to Series B	Yearly	– Numbers insured against unemployment	– Ministers – Departmental officials
5) Series C	Monthly	Statistics relating to the Armed Forces and auxiliary services: – Strength of the Armed Forces – Civil Defence Services – Women's Services	– Departmental officials – Ministers
6) Series D	Monthly	Statistics relating to production and man-power – Naval construction – Output of ground weapons – Aircraft – Supplies to Russia – Manpower for munitions industries	– Ministers

	Period of issue	Contents	Circulation
7) Series E	Monthly	Statistics relating to import problems: – Employment of shipping – Round voyage and turn-round times – Repairs – Losses and new construction of ships – Losses of goods at sea – Imports	– Ministers – Shipping Committee – Departmental officials
8) Series F	Monthly	Statistics relating to tankers and petroleum products: – Employment of tankers – Round voyage and turn-round times – Repairs – Losses and new construction – Imports – Petroleum products: output consumption stocks	– Ministers – Oil Control Board – Departmental officials

B. STATEMENTS RELATING TO MUNITIONS PRODUCTION

	Period of issue	Contents	Circulation
9) United Kingdom, United States, Canada and Eastern Group Munitions Production	Monthly	Actual and estimated future production of munitions, warlike stores and merchant shipping by: – United Kingdom, – USA, – Canada, – Australia, – India, – New Zealand and – South Africa	– Ministry of Production – Production and Services Departments – United States Administration.
10) Analysis of United Kingdom Output	Monthly	Actual and estimated production of Admiralty, Ministry of Supply and Ministry of Aircraft Production	– Ministry of Production – Production and Services Departments – United States Administration.
11) Analysis of United States Output	Monthly	Official munitions production of the United States (actual and forecast)	– Ministry of Production – Production and Services Departments

C. STATEMENTS RELATING TO STOCKS OF MUNITIONS

	Period of issue	Contents	Circulation
12) Army and SAA Stocks Statement	Monthly	Establishment and reserve stocks, geographical distribution and surplus or deficiency of army weapons and ammunition	War Office Ministry of Production Joint Staff Mission
13) Aircraft Stocks and Movements	Monthly	Stocks, geographical distribution and movements of aircraft classified by type	Air Ministry Admiralty Ministry of Production Ministry of Aircraft Production Joint Staff Mission
14) Naval Stocks	Monthly	Stocks of naval vessels classified by type. (The editions for March, June, September and December included stocks of naval weapons and ammunition.)	Admiralty Ministry of Production Joint Staff Mission

D. STATEMENTS RELATING TO MUNITIONS ASSIGNMENTS AND ALLOCATIONS

	Period of issue	Contents	Circulation
15) Schedule of Assignments, Allocations and Shipments	Monthly	Army weapons, equipment and ammunition: Assignments from the – UK – USA – Canada – Australia Allocations and shipments to various countries and theatres of war	– London Munitions Assignment Board Army Assignment Sub-committee – Ministry of Production – Dominions Office – Joint Staff Mission
16) Naval Assignments and Allocations	Quarterly	Assignments and allocations – Ordnance equipment – Torpedoes – Ammunition – Marine engines – Naval aircraft	– Admiralty – Ministry of Production – Joint Staff Mission

E. GENERAL STATISTICAL STATEMENTS

	Period of issue	Contents	Circulation
17) Stocks of food and animal feeding stuffs, raw materials and petroleum products	Monthly	Statistics and charts of stocks, including forecasts for next three months	– Lord President's Committee – Shipping Committee
18) Imports under Departmental Programmes	Ten-daily	Statistics of imports – Food – Raw materials – Tanker	– Ministers – Departmental officials
19) Statistics relating to Iron and Steel	Monthly	Production, imports, consumption and stocks of iron and steel	– Ministers – Departmental officials
20) Statistics relating to strengths and battle casualties	Monthly	Strength and battle casualties of armed forces of UK and Dominions	– Chiefs of Staff – Departmental officials
21) Standard statement of gains and losses of merchant ships outside enemy control	Weekly	Gains and losses of ocean-going merchant ships	– British Shipping Mission, Washington – United States Administration

F. ANNUAL STATEMENTS RELATING TO
WAR FINANCE AND NATIONAL INCOME AND EXPENDITURE

22) An analysis of the sources of war finance and an estimate of national income and expenditure 1938–40.
Command 6261, 1941

23) An analysis of the sources of war finance and an estimate of national income and expenditure 1938–40 and 1941.
Command 6347, April 1942

INDEX

A

B

C

D

E